Taking
the
Lead

What Riding a Bike
Can Teach You
About Leadership

Damian Gerke

ISBN-10: 1537094157
ISBN-13: 9781537094151

PRAISE FOR *TAKING THE LEAD*

"If leadership is like a bicycle, then *Taking the Lead* is the key to removing your training wheels! Filled with both common sense and profound insights, Damian Gerke makes sure that you're ready for the leadership road ahead."

— AmyK Hutchens,
speaker, business strategist and Intelligence Activist,
AmyK International, author of *The Secrets Leaders Keep*

"*Taking the Lead* covers almost every aspect of leadership, yet is one of the most readable and practical books on the subject you'll find anywhere. It takes the mystery out of leadership and gives you concrete ideas for how to become a better leader."

— Kevin Oakes,
CEO, Institute for Corporate Productivity (i4cp)

"In *Taking the Lead*, Damian Gerke poignantly links bike riding with leadership in a way that draws the reader in. The biking stories are fascinating and are directly related to being a leader. Throughout the book, there is learning about both!"

— Linda Miller,
Global Liaison for Coaching,
The Ken Blanchard Companies

"I found *Taking the Lead* to be a captivating and amazingly comprehensive primer on leadership—even though I'm not a cyclist. Damian Gerke's passions for leadership coaching and cycling resonate throughout, making his book a joy to read and readily applicable. Not only does it inspire me to be a better leader, but to also get out there and ride!"

— C. Scott Franklin,
President/CEO, Lanier Upshaw, Inc.,
Naval Academy graduate and former naval aviator

"Whether you are a young leader looking to move to the next level or an experienced leader working to become great at influencing others, *Taking the Lead* will provide you with the direction, insight and knowledge to gain the skills you need to achieve your leadership goals."

— Jeff Chamberlain,
Vice President of Real Estate,
Publix Supermarkets, Inc.

"Damian's take on leadership and drawing the corollary with riding a bike has produced a very interesting read. In particular, I applaud the chapter on the importance of understanding a leader's 'fit' with the culture. My 40 years of leadership experience, both inside and outside the business world, has revealed the truth that success as a leader is situational: If you want to succeed, you must be able to recognize how best to adapt your leadership style to the environment. This book successfully paints that picture. *Taking the Lead* is both a pleasure to read and a solid resource to improve as a leader."

— Cliff Otto,
CEO, Saddle Creek Logistics Services

"They say that once you've learned how to ride a bike, you never forget. In *Taking the Lead*, Damian Gerke uses his cycling experiences to make some very memorable and important points about what it means to be an effective leader. If you take the time to read this great little book, you won't forget its lessons."

— Scott Eblin,
executive coach, author of *The Next Level* and
Overworked and Overwhelmed: The Mindfulness Alternative

"*Taking the Lead* offers practical and comprehensive insights on leadership. This well-written and easy-to-read book shows how to effectively confront thorny situations while staying balanced and on track."

— Dr. Mary Lippitt,
President of Enterprise Management Ltd.,
author of *Brilliant or Blunder: 6 Ways Leaders
Navigate Uncertainty, Opportunity and Complexity*

"*Taking the Lead* is refreshing, approachable, and empowering! You'll find the juxtaposition of cycling and leadership both engaging and thought provoking—whether you are an avid cyclist or haven't been on a bicycle for a long time. This is a book for someone who wants to take their leadership skills to the next level. It is filled with actionable tools that will power your ride on the road to leadership effectiveness!"

— **Joseph Michelli,**
New York Times #1 best-selling author of books like
Driven to Delight, Leading the Starbucks Way,
The Zappos Experience and *The New Gold Standard*

"Wow, I really enjoyed *Taking the Lead.* There are so many great leadership connections delivered in such a powerful way. We see a ton of leadership books in the market, but this book is worth every minute of time spent reading it!"

— **Larry Linne,**
former NFL player,
CEO of InCite Performance Group

To Cheryl

My beloved bride, partner, lover, friend and confidant

CONTENTS

ACKNOWLEDGMENTS

Writing a book may seem like a solitary endeavor, but it is far from it; it takes a team. There are so many people who have invested in me and whose influences have made this book a reality. First, from a writing perspective, I want to thank my family. They have believed in and challenged me to improve. They never rolled their eyes at the thought of Dad as a writer. Their support has encouraged me beyond words. I also think of the people who endured my early writing and lovingly but forcefully challenged me to raise the bar. Dr. Bob Pyne and Natalie Olsen come to mind.

Next, from a leadership perspective, there have been so many people who inspired me, and brought clarity and reality to leadership concepts that were untouchable aches and unscratchable itches. Their own passionate search for (and living examples of) *Semper Incito* and leadership excellence became my own: Bill Hybels, Dave Logan, Ron Donnini, Del Poling, Randy Frazee and Norman LeClair.

To the folks directly involved in this project, I can't thank you enough for your investment of time and energy. Your fingerprints are all over it. Particular thanks go to Ruth Barnes, whose unique position as both a leader and an editor gave this book a much-needed boost of credibility in its early stages. The end results would have been chaotic without you. Thanks to my editor Misann Ellmaker for the consistency of thought and her unique ability to offer substance without affecting style—and for putting up with my endless confusion over the proper use of commas. Thanks as well to Rick Fidanzato, not only for his assistance on this project but also for his insight into cycling and his hunger to get better as a leader. It's folks like you who make coaching a success! And thanks to Amy with Allen Harris Design for contributing her gift of artistic design and, more importantly, for her friendship and encouragement—and to Yvonne who put up with me in creating the website. You both are amazing!

Finally, thanks to God for the inspiration and abilities you have given me. It would all be purposeless without you. SDG!

INTRODUCTION

*"The greatest danger for most of us is not that
our aim is too high and we miss it,
but that it is too low and we reach it."*
Michelangelo

Leadership.

That people continue to write about leadership tells me two things.

First, leadership matters. Nothing of any significance in human history has ever happened without it. When it's well-applied, leadership transforms lives, organizations, families and societies. Leadership is the object of study, critique and fascination. So we pursue it—passionately.

Second, leadership is a mystery. It's not a formula, a list of paint-by-number steps or a scripted process. If it were, someone would have figured it out by now. Leadership is like art: It might be hard to define, but you know it when you see it.

There's another thing that leadership is like: riding a bike.

The cycling/leadership comparison works on a couple of levels. I'm a novice rider. Having taken up cycling in the second half of life, I will never compete in the Tour de France (though I've got a good shot at wearing the yellow jersey in the Tour de My Neighborhood). Yet, I'm smitten. There's something about time in the saddle that clears the head, heals the spirit and satisfies the soul. Whatever it is, I'm hooked. I'm a bike fan(atic).

> **"Leadership is like art: It might be hard to define, but you know it when you see it."**

I'm also a leadership fan(atic). I know my own leadership competencies well enough to recognize that I'm not suited to be a corporate leader. But I take great satisfaction in being a trusted advisor to those who are—and that's where my greatest strengths lie. As a student of leadership, I have developed some insight and competency in creating leadership excellence in others.

Beyond helping other leaders improve their craft, the opportunity for my own development compels me. I want to get better at it. I wish I could go back and revisit all those leadership opportunities I either missed or messed up. But life, like a bike, doesn't go backwards. So I move forward, applying the lessons learned as best I can to the road I'm on now.

In both cycling and leadership, I'm learning. Both have an elusive level of perfection. What's the perfect bike ride? Even the best rides I've been on have raised the bar, calling me to another level that is close enough to taste yet tantalizingly just beyond reach. Leadership has that same quality. It's never perfected; you never "arrive." Its limits are unexplored like a horizon calling you to stretch a little further. Even as you cover new ground, you realize there's still further you can go.

> "Leadership ... [is] never perfected; you never 'arrive.' Its limits are unexplored like a horizon calling you to stretch a little further."

Yet with all its mystery, leadership is also curiously common. The stuff of quality leadership can be seen throughout the human experience. It's revealed in virtually every social interaction—big and small, formal or informal. It's much closer than we think and can be as simple and basic as riding a bike.

As a case in point, I offer this book.

I invite you to discover what I mean about leadership being a common sense reality. I've seen leadership principles come to life through the miles of my biking experience. In reading this, I hope you'll be motivated to apply these principles in your life on whatever road you may be riding.

Everyone has the opportunity to lead because leadership is desperately needed at almost every level of human organization:

families, companies, schools, non-profit organizations, neighborhoods, churches, committees, nations ... You name it, great leadership is called for. In fact, I believe most of the social ills we wrestle with come from ineffective leadership.

You don't have to be a professional cyclist to ride a bike. Neither do you have to be a CEO to lead. Start now. Commit to growing and developing your leadership with the pedal strokes of each conversation you have. The more you practice leadership, the better leader you'll become.

Just as you won't improve your biking performance if all you do is watch the Tour de France on TV, you won't become a better leader if all you do is read a book on the subject and get the author's perspective. Leadership must be pursued, embraced and tried on for size to become real in your life.

It takes an attitude, a drive; it takes commitment to get up and go riding. It requires an "always forward" attitude. This phrase has great significance for me. So much so that I had it painted on my bike in Latin: *Semper Incito.* People usually get the "semper" part, thanks to the motto of the U.S. Marines: *Semper Fideles,* "always faithful."

"Incito," however, almost always draws a blank. It's Latin for "forward," but it's much more than a direction. It's also an action: It can be translated as "to urge on or spur"—as in "to incite." It implies quickening, inspiring or motivating and igniting a fire. It means to bring increase or to build up.

> "Leadership must be pursued, embraced and tried on for size to become real in your life."

Forward/incito is a biking term. Riders think "forward," and every action they take on the bike is designed to move them there.

Forward/incito is a leadership term. Leaders think "forward," and every action they take is designed to move their team there.

In that sense, excellence in leadership isn't given to you. It must be taken. My hope is the stories in this book help you get better at taking the lead—no matter where you are on your leadership journey.

My first priority in laying out this book was to make it readable. Each chapter stands on its own, without sequence or prerequisite. So feel free to jump to the topics that interest or challenge you most and come back to the remaining topics.

> "If you haven't thought about your legacy as a person and a leader, you're riding with one eye closed."

I fully expect some will disagree with some points I make. There is a lot of room for different views in this conversation, and my hope is you come away with clearer thoughts and a crystalized approach to improving your leadership performance.

I also encourage you to read the Epilogue. If you haven't thought about your legacy as a person and a leader, you're riding with one eye closed. More than anything else, this may change what you do to take the lead.

It comes to this: The road is before you. Are you ready to take the lead?

1 – GO WITH WHAT YOU GOT

*"You've got to think about big things
while you're doing small things, so that
all the small things go in the right direction."*
Alvin Toffler

"Damian, that's … an interesting bike." One of the riders with the St. Petersburg Bicycle Club was making conversation on a group ride, while we were stopped at a red light.

"Yeah …" I agreed and not knowing what else to say, "I guess it is."

I began my cycling life on a hand-me-down mountain bike—a 1992 Bridgestone MB-6 that I outfitted with road tires and converted into a hybrid. It was a respectable bike back in the day, but its day was quite a while ago.

> "The Beast trained me. It tasked me to work harder and to push myself when it was more convenient to complain."

The bike was a gift from my brother-in-law Stewart. Actually, the bike belonged to his wife Robyn, who (like me) is eight inches shorter than Stewart. I'd wanted to see if cycling was for me and wanted to spend as little money as possible trying to figure that out. As life got crazy, I never got the chance. Six moves, two countries, three kids and two spinal surgeries later, the bike still sat in my garage, largely unused.

I finally decided it was now or never. My surgeries had eliminated any fitness exercise involving impact. Serious weightlifting and running were out. The alternative—doing nothing—was fast becoming the worst possible thing for me.

I didn't know what to expect. Cycling seemed like an expensive version of distance running, which I'd always considered tortuous. I never had the endurance for it, and frankly, I always found it monotonous. "Running" and "high" were two words that don't go together for me.

The bike had a steel frame built to take the rigors of mountain trails. By today's road bike weight standards, it was a beast, tipping the scales at 33 pounds. A good road bike weighs half that.

The Beast was outfitted with 18 gear combinations, with three sprockets in front and six in back. This sounds like a lot, but since it was geared as a mountain bike, most of the gears were useless on flat Florida roads. 99% of the time, I only used three gears.

The tires were wide—twice as wide as road tires—which meant more friction. The harder I pedaled, the more it worked against me. The wheels were also smaller in diameter, which further limited speed.

The Beast was outfitted with a set of flat bar handlebars, offering few options for positioning my hands. Grasping the ends of the bar placed my hands in a non-neutral position and added to road fatigue.

All of this may sound like whining, but over many miles, it adds up to a lot more work than necessary.

> "Challenges and limitations can be reasons to complain, or they can be opportunities to get better. If we fixate on what we don't have, we resent and mismanage what we do have."

On every ride, I was faced with the reality that my equipment wasn't the best. It didn't bother me at first, but then I began to resent it. It became an excuse not to ride or push myself to improve. We had decided to wait on purchasing a new bike until we got some medical bills paid off. So it was either ride the Beast or have it sit in my garage. Again.

I chose to ride.

We all want more stuff, newer stuff and better opportunities. It's human nature to be frustrated with the limitations of our current circumstances. That's why advertising is so effective: *Get this product, and your life will be better. The grass is greener over here, and it's only one click away.*

But in leadership—as in most areas of life—you have a choice: Challenges and limitations can be reasons to complain, or they can be opportunities to get better. If we fixate on what we don't have, we resent and mismanage what we do have.

I'm not just putting a happy spin on things. The Beast trained me. The extra weight forced me into shape. It tasked me to work harder and to push myself when it was more convenient to complain.

The reality is it's not about the bike. It's about the heart, the drive, the passion, the consistency and the commitment. There will always be lighter bikes and newer models with more technology and the latest materials.

I knew I'd eventually get a new bike; a real bike. But until I did, I committed to getting the most out of the Beast. In my mind, if I couldn't get the best out of my current situation, how would I ever get the best out of the ideal one?

> "Leadership is, in part, a stewardship. It's managing and leveraging opportunities, getting the best possible results out of the resources available to you."

There may be other leadership opportunities in your future that may match up better with your style and experience and personality. But remember, "better" opportunities often aren't easier. And any position with more responsibility means the challenges are greater: The risks are higher, the margins are tighter and the consequences are more significant.

Leadership is, in part, stewardship. It's managing and leveraging opportunities, getting the best possible results out of the resources available to you.

Lead now, where you are. Deal with your circumstances, your limitations and resource shortfalls. Squeeze out every last mph you can. Don't resent it. Lean into it—embrace it.

Pursue it.

Know it.

Appreciate it.

It's training you.

Put It in Motion

- **Change Your Perspective.** Don't resent a leadership opportunity just because it's a challenge. Embrace it because it's shaping your leadership; it's making you better.

- **Focus on Results and Getting Better.** If you can't get the best out of your current leadership opportunity, how do you expect to get the best out of your "ideal" leadership opportunity (if there even is such a thing)?

- **Don't Fall Into the Resentment Trap.** Resentment only breeds unproductive thoughts and nasty attitudes. Stay positive, and you can—and will—make a difference.

---

2 – FIT HAPPENS

*"To the person who does not know where he wants to go
there is no favorable wind."*
Seneca

Bikes come in all shapes and sizes. It's a good thing because humans do too.

Beyond the obvious variety in frame size—after all, you should be able to straddle your bike without, ahem, discomfort—there are a myriad of details that impact the fit between bike and rider. It's all about the geometry: leg, arm and torso length, curvature of the spine and flexibility of the legs and hips. Then there are the multiple combinations of frame angles and positioning of the seat, handlebar and pedals. When you've been fitted, all the angles are set up to get the most power out of your body geometry. You don't have to reach, stretch, strain or contort.

It just fits.

Of course, if your rides are limited to the occasional trip around the block, fit is not a major issue. But when you're riding habits are more serious and your goal is sustained effectiveness and success over many hours and miles, fitting with your bike makes all the difference in the world. In a head-to-head race with all other things being equal, better fit beats the better rider—every time.

> *"...better fit beats
> the better rider
> —every time."*

Riding a bike that is not fit to you is an across-the-board budget cut in your power and efficiency. You get penalized with every pedal stroke. You also stand the real chance of injuring yourself from making your body strain unnecessarily.

The bottom line is you can't just hop on any bike and expect to be competitive over the long haul.

On my first bike (if you didn't read it yet, see Chapter 1 for more details on "the Beast"), I was limited on the fit adjustments I could make. I wanted to invest as little as possible since it was a test bike. The frame was the right size, but its mountain bike geometry was not ideal for road cycling. I had to work with the other components to get the best fit possible.

The same is true with leadership. There are many aspects to an organization that determine a good "fit." Expectations, management approach (both how you're managed and how you manage others), history, culture, how things get done, operations, processes, goals and objectives, who you're teamed with—they're all part of the unique geometry of your role. Their positioning will make your fit either comfortable or miserable.

> **"Culture eats strategy for breakfast."**
>
> *Henry Ford*

As was the case with the Beast, the options for fit adjustment may be limited in your current role. Perhaps you got transferred or promoted into a role with a different fit. Or maybe you're experiencing the culture shock of corporate acquisition where the expectations and the processes have all shifted.

While it may appear that you're stuck with this geometry, you may have more opportunity to create a workable fit than you realize. For instance, the expected outcomes are often fixed but how you produce those results is usually not. It's easy for people to presume only one way of doing things (i.e. "the way we've always done it"), with little thought given to creativity or innovation. This is your opportunity. You should always be aware of what the typical processes are and what you can do to tweak, alter or change them outright. The more you can adjust them to optimize your fit, the better off you'll be.

One of the best resources I've run across for issues of a role fit is Marcus Buckingham's *The One Thing You Need to Know*. Check out the last section where he presents how to achieve sustained success. It alone is worth the price of the book. He gives you several ways to adjust your role to achieve the best possible fit and make the role work for you.

Another great resource is *The First 90 Days*. Michael Watkins wrote this book with new employee onboarding in mind, and he examines how to return value in the first 90 days of a new role. Of particular note is how he distinguishes organizations and roles in terms of their business state: startups, turn-arounds, realignments or sustaining success. I find that leaders often fail to recognize the state of their role and blindly proceed with the same approach that brought them success in the past.

The fit process was reversed with my second bike. I now had the opportunity to choose a bike that fit me and my riding goals. Dialing in the fit while riding the bike on a stationary trainer made all the difference in the world. I could observe myself in the mirrors and see the impact of minor adjustments. I knew these would result in major differences out on the road.

> "...the real values (which may be different from the stated values)— reveal themselves. They're not hard to find, if you know what to look for."

When considering other leadership opportunities, you should look toward the one that best fits you. Assess the role and the organization/department before you get into the role. As with cycling, if you're looking to ride on unpaved trails in the mountains you shouldn't be looking at triathlon bikes.

All this, of course, requires that you know yourself well enough to know what the best fit is. Some leaders are more entrepreneurial by nature. Others are developers. Some are set up for an innovative environment. Others have the political savvy and sense of timing to manage realignments or the ability to take a successful situation and make it better without blowing it up. The better you know your own leadership "geometry"—the size and shape of all your most effective behaviors—the better chance you have of insuring a good fit.

Even when the industry is a fit and the role lines up well with your personal leadership style, there's one more thing you must consider: values.

When I was looking for the bike that would give me the best fit, it was important to me to build a partnership with someone who'd be an ongoing resource for me. I wanted someone who'd support my goals and continued improvement. I wanted more than "a good deal" on a bike and wasn't interested in working with someone whose primary interest was moving some inventory. I wanted someone who shared my values about cycling.

That person for me is Rick Fidanzato, owner of the Trek Store in St. Petersburg, FL. That Rick operates one of the top-performing Trek stores in the country speaks to his qualifications as a cycling resource. Clearly, he knows bikes.

> "The values of both the organization and its leaders are the biggest determining factors when it comes to fit."

But it's the similarity of our personal values and perspectives on cycling that makes him such a valuable resource. For obvious reasons, Rick wants to sell bikes—he couldn't sustain and grow his business if he didn't. But the culture of Rick's business is built around serving his customers and helping them experience the pleasure and health benefits of riding their bikes. Listen to Rick talk about it—even for just a few minutes—and you'll see it: Getting a sale without doing all he can to support the customer's lifestyle is a cop out. It violates his values. He can't do it and sleep comfortably at night.

That's why I know I can trust him when he talks to me about my bike.

The values of both the organization and its leaders are the biggest determining factors when it comes to fit. Ultimately, values—the real values (which may be different from the stated values)—reveal themselves. They're not hard to find if you know what to look for. I hit values again in Chapter 18 – Know Who You Are (And Who You're Not), but I also encourage you to check out *Tribal Leadership* by Dave Logan and his team. It will help you assess values and understand how they shape organizational culture. It will help you understand how to leverage them for action and—most importantly—to build strategy around values.

As Henry Ford said, "Culture eats strategy for breakfast." It has a higher correlation to success than things like leadership style, strategy details, vision clarity/quality, market share or technology. That's because culture *interprets* strategy. If a good strategy aligns with the culture, the strategy produces good results. If it does not, the strategy won't fit the organization; it won't resonate with anyone. It will come across as trite, hype, fake, foreign or any number of other negative interpretations. It will not be accepted, embraced and owned—and it will produce poor results.

In their book *Corporate Culture and Performance,* John Kotter and James Heskett unpack the results of an 11-year study of corporate financial performance. The results showed that companies with healthy cultures that highly valued employees, customers, and owners, and that encouraged leadership across all levels of the organization outperformed companies that did not have a healthy culture. In almost every important growth category—revenue, employment, stock price and net income—the differences were staggering, including a difference in equity value of 827%.

Culture is complex, but the biggest component of culture is organizational values. If the values are healthy, compelling and prominent in the organization, the culture will more than likely be strong. But more importantly, if your leadership values don't align with the organization's values, you'll face an uphill, uncomfortable, outsider's battle to influence the organization.

The better fit beats the better rider—every time.

Put It in Motion

- **Determine Your Best Leadership Approach.** Your role should vary according to the situation: Startup, turn-around, realignment or sustaining success.

- **The Better Fit Beats the Stronger Leader.** If you have the option, look for a situation that aligns with your values, leadership style, passions and interests. You'll go further, faster, and it'll be much more fun.

- **Values are Real.** Every organization has values. Not every organization is aware of their true values, and even fewer are intentional about operating by them. That's something to think about when you consider that culture has a stronger correlation to success than strategy.

- **Remember: Culture *Interprets* Strategy.** If a good strategy aligns with the culture, the strategy produces good results. If it does not, it won't "fit" the organization.

- **Let Values Do the Heavy Lifting.** Everything becomes clearer and easier when your values are working for you. Do whatever you can to identify them and then operate by them.

---

3 – KNOW YOUR SURROUNDINGS

"The best educated human being is the one who understands most about the life in which he is placed."
Helen Keller

Bike riders have a saying: "It's okay to get *caught* in the rain, but we don't *ride* in the rain." In addition to requiring a time-consuming detail (bike cleaning), riding in the rain has a couple of consequences—neither of which is good.

For one, it's rough on the equipment. Water (and the mud that comes with it) works against the gears, chain and derailleurs (the mechanisms that change the gears). Keeping these properly lubed is critical to operating effectively and to longer life. Wet tires attract sand and grit, which erodes the rubber and contributes to blowouts. And water on the rims makes braking unpredictable.

> "As a leader, you must never assume that what worked in your last role will work in your current role."

Another issue is loss of traction. Losing contact with the road, even at marginal speeds, can be a scary prospect. Crashing your bike—the bane of cycling—is both embarrassing and dangerous. It's also potentially expensive: When decent composite frames run well north of $2,000, it's definitely a party you want to skip.

Summers in Florida usually involve rain—the thunderstorm variety. In fact, Tampa Bay has the highest lightning strike density in the U.S. (believe me, our professional hockey team is aptly named). Thunderstorms in Florida are rarely associated with cold fronts as they are in the rest of the country. Here, they are daily summer events. The sea breeze collides with the air mass over land,

---

pushing the warm, moist air aloft and creating random, powerful thunderheads. You're usually pretty safe riding in the mornings. But around 3:00, there's a cumulonimbus popping up somewhere in the Bay Area, which makes afternoon riding a crapshoot.

After living in Florida for over a decade, I've learned to read these patterns. Knowing the wind patterns ahead of time, you can often read the clouds and anticipate how things are going to form. But that's not enough. You have to actively keep an eye on your surroundings.

> "…you must know your surroundings and read the obvious (and the often not-so-obvious) weather' patterns…"

One time I rode out under a clear, summer sky. But when I turned around for the inbound leg of my ride, I was surprised by a dark and angry sky that had been building behind me. I pushed hard to get back home but didn't make it before rain was falling in buckets and lightning was popping all around me. I had to find a place to hole up and wait it out.

I got home late, wet and hungry.

Leadership has an equivalent process. To be an effective leader, you must know your surroundings and read the obvious (and the often not-so-obvious) "weather" patterns: certain cultural elements, relationship patterns, history, tendencies, politics, perspectives, assumptions … a host of things that together create a unique organizational environment.

If you miss these patterns, you end up getting caught in storms unnecessarily. Angry and formidable events can build behind you when you're not looking. You can easily find yourself vulnerable to lightning popping all around, and you have to work to position yourself so you aren't exposed.

Even worse, you may be the cause of storms. Don't misunderstand me. Some leader-induced storms are beneficial and healthy for the organization. After all, leadership usually involves change and addressing under-performance or ineffective processes. To not confront these things is to miss the leadership opportunity.

But other leader-induced storms are needless, counter-productive and distracting. Maybe it's from turning up the heat unnecessarily high; maybe it's the level of change you're creating by trying to do too much, too fast. These storms do no one any good and should usually be avoided. Knowing your surroundings will help you determine how much heat to add, when to dial it back and which direction you should be pushing.

The last thing you want to do is assume that all weather is the same. I've lived in Arkansas, Texas, the Pacific Northwest, the high desert of southern California and the Midwest before living in Florida. All of these locations had storms, each with their own (even violent) hazards. But the storms in each region were entirely different.

As a leader, you must never assume that what worked in your last role will work in your current role. Each is different, and you must keep a look out for the unique environmental clues in order to avoid getting caught in an angry storm that could have been avoided.

> "Some leader-induced storms are beneficial and healthy for the organization ... But [others] are unnecessary, counter-productive and distracting."

A 2004 MIT Sloan School of Management study on CEO failure noted a pattern with new CEO misfires that resulted in billions of dollars of lost value, including such high-profile companies as Coca-Cola, Lucent, Xerox and Proctor and Gamble.[1] They drew a critical distinction between leadership tendencies:

> Content-oriented CEOs focus on the substance of the company's business. ... In contrast, context-oriented CEOs focus more intensely on the environment in which content decisions are made.

> Once the incumbents departed ... and the new CEOs suddenly had to create a new context on their own, trouble started. ... They often fell back on their historic strengths, which were of limited use in the CEO role. Ultimately, the combination of declining performance and

---

[1] Conger, Jay A., Nadler, David A. "When CEOs Step Up To Fail." *Harvard Business Review* Spring 2004. Vol. 45 No. 3. Web.

increasing disaffection within the top leadership groups became painfully evident to the boards of directors, which removed the CEOs.

Remember, *Semper Incito.* You lead in the present tense; you and those you lead live in *today's* context. Go back to the past for wisdom and perspective, but lead in the environment of the moment.

Put It in Motion

- **Learn the "Weather" Patterns in Your Organization.** Every organization (like regions of the country) tends to have different patterns in storms: things like history, unwritten rules, pet projects or topics, etc. Dismiss these at your own peril.

- **Don't Cause Unnecessary Storms.** Change is part of what leaders do, but make sure the change is purposeful. Don't change things just for the sake of change.

- **Don't Depend Too Heavily on the Past.** Though it may look similar, the environment you're in today is likely very different from previous environments. Lead in the present tense. Look for clues in your current environment to ensure you're aware of everything that's going on around you today.

---

4 – PREPARE

"Hope is not a plan."
Steve Adubato

My midweek rides usually come after work. Even with a nice trail convenient to my workplace, getting a ride in during the week is tough because I'm limited by the approaching sunset. Many committed cyclists don't mind riding in the dark, but I've never had a comfort level for it. Not being able to see obstacles and debris on the road is never a good thing. Even worse is not being visible to pedestrians or motorists. Riding in the dark introduces a level of anxiety that, for me, takes away from the joy of riding.

Since I usually end up with about an hour's worth of useable daylight on weekday rides, I use them as time trials. I ride out hard and fast for 30 minutes and then try to beat my time on the return leg. It's a good way to increase strength and diversity into my riding experience since it complements my longer rides on the weekend.

> "Give me six hours to chop down a tree, and I will spend the first four sharpening the axe."
>
> *Abraham Lincoln*

Because time is short, it's tempting to jump on the bike and ride but doing so will cause more harm than good. I've gotten serious cramps from not stretching properly, and I've strained my knees from not warming up, resulting in tendonitis that takes weeks to go away. You're also asking for trouble when you take your heart from sedentary to immediately pushing the upper limits of your cardio range.

So midweek rides always come with competing pressures: Act (so you won't lose your opportunity) vs. prepare (so you'll be in position to make the most of your opportunity).

One of the greatest realities leaders face is the immediacy of their role. Leaders must act *now;* delay means lost opportunity. The pace of the world we live in, along with the fact that we're always pushed to do more with less, means that life comes at you fast. Like it or not, I don't see this changing.

Ever been in a situation where you were unprepared? When a task, challenge, question or responsibility got thrown at you and—without background, history or context—you had to make a critical decision about it?

> "[Preparing is] the leadership equivalent to 'putting on your own oxygen mask first, before assisting others with their mask.'"

And how about those situations you were prepared for: Confident. Quick. Decisive. Unsurprised. Sharp.

Which condition would you prefer to consistently operate in?

Preparation in leadership works the same way. Granted, you can't prepare for every eventuality, and at times, you have to act on instincts alone. Sometimes you have to wing it. But sometimes shouldn't be all the time.

Abraham Lincoln got it right when he said, "Give me six hours to chop down a tree, and I will spend the first four sharpening the axe." This is the idea behind preparing as a leader. It's the leadership equivalent to "putting on your own oxygen mask first, before assisting others with their mask." If you're not prepared, people won't be able to count on you when the time comes to act.

I've seen a couple of areas of preparation bring particularly strong dividends in leadership: fitness and planning.

Fitness: Get Fit, and Stay Fit

When it comes to fitness preparation and riding a bike, there are some basic things you have to do: hydrate, stretch, warm up and consistently eat right. Your body is an amazing piece of electromechanical equipment: intricate and delicate, yet incredibly adaptive and flexible. Like any other piece of equipment, it requires regular maintenance to operate with peak efficiency and effectiveness. If you don't maintain the machine, it will break down.

According to the American Heart Association[2], the leading cause of death and workplace disability are cardiovascular conditions such as heart disease, stroke, hypertension, heart rhythm disorders, peripheral artery disease and heart failure. They account for 30% of all medical costs that U.S. companies will encounter—a staggering $314 billion in direct costs, to say nothing of the estimated $160 billion in lost productivity. These come from risk factors that are often avoidable: smoking, excess weight, physical inactivity, high blood pressure, high cholesterol and diabetes.

Here's the deal when it comes to leadership and fitness: Your influence increases with practice and wisdom. Wise, effective leadership behavior is honed and cultivated as it's practiced over time. Getting fit—and staying fit—puts you in position to continually hone your leadership craft.

When it comes to leadership and fitness, the main concerns are usually pretty basic—but the basics make all the difference:

- Eat well
- Get enough sleep
- Do regular physical activity

> "Your body is an amazing piece of electromechanical equipment: intricate and delicate, but at the same time incredibly adaptive and flexible."

Your body's fuel comes from what you eat. If you put in junk, how can you realistically expect it to function properly? It needs good nutrition. And getting the right supplements is essential. The typical American simply doesn't get the right kind of nutrition from the processed foods currently in our diet.

Sleep is another key. It's the reset button for your body. Without sleep, the digestive system becomes less effective, the immune system gets weak and blood pressure goes up. You'll be stressing your body.

Getting enough sleep can be tough since there's almost always more to do than there is time to do it. There are two concerns:

---

[2] Carnethon, Mercedes, et al. *Worksite Wellness Programs for Cardiovascular Disease Prevention: A Policy Statement from The American Heart Association.* Oct. 27, 2009. PDF file.

amount and consistency. We need sufficient and patterned sleep so our bodies can establish a rhythm.

When it comes to exercise, it doesn't have to be much, but it should be regular. You really *can* afford to stretch 10 minutes a day. You *can* squeeze in 30 minutes of some activity three times a week: walking, light exercise like push-ups or some strength-building. Almost *anything* works, but you have to do *something*. I've seen enough results from yoga to know it's extremely valuable, and it adds a flexibility component most other exercise programs ignore. Plus it's simple enough to do it at home or on the road in your hotel room.

So do you want to be influential for the long run? Or do you want to handicap yourself and undercut your leadership by not preparing—guaranteeing you'll be less effective?

> "Do you want to be the North Star or a shooting star?"

Do you want to leave a legacy; or do you want to be remembered as a flash-in-the-pan, could-have-been, one-time wonder, where-is-she-now leader?

Do you want to be the North Star or a shooting star?

The choice, quite literally, is yours. And failing to choose—to delay or put off—is choosing to fail as a leader.

Planning

There are some basic steps to take before each ride. You conduct an equipment check: Top off your tires with the right pressure. Reset your trip computer. Don't forget your spare tube. Do a visual check of things like the brakes, the chain.

Then there's the planning step: Where are we riding today? How long will it be? Do we know when and where we're turning around? And you should create expectations for the ride: Is this a casual ride? Are we building up endurance? Are we prepared for a high pace?

The point is this: It almost never makes sense to hop on the bike and ride without knowing where you're going and how you're going to get there.

The same is true for leadership: Leaders should plan. Be clear about the destination. Create expectations about the path(s) you'll take to get there. Estimate the costs, and the energy required for achievement. Think ahead about where things might go wrong and about where unexpected challenges might show up. Create what-if scenarios and play out possible solutions in advance.

The way the marketplace (and life in general) is going, it's natural that both the level and complexity of stuff getting thrown at us is increasing. It's easy to find yourself in a reactive posture, where you don't really plan, you just react. This is, obviously, not a good position to be in long-term. In general, if you find your activity to be mostly reactionary, then it's probably a good bet that you need more—or perhaps different—planning.

You want to be as prepared as possible to handle issues that come up, and one important way to be prepared is to consider them in advance.

Put It in Motion

- **Put On Your Own Oxygen Mask Before Helping Others.** If you're not prepared, people won't be able to count on you when the time comes to act.

- **Don't Neglect Your Fitness.** Eating well, getting enough sleep and having some regular physical activity will put you in a better position to lead more effectively. Neglecting it only invites a meltdown.

- **Plan.** Don't allow yourself to be in reaction mode all the time. Make sure you're as clear as you can be on the destination, how you want to get there and the possible detours you may have to take.

5 – WHEN YOU'RE ON THE STREET, YOU GOTTA ACT LIKE A CAR

"Being a leader is like being a lady.
If you have to tell people you are one,
you probably aren't."
Margaret Thatcher

First Street North in St. Petersburg is a popular road for cyclists. It's long, wide and doesn't have many stoplights. And without a convenient connection at either the north or south end, it's not a major artery for north-south traffic, meaning vehicle traffic on First Street is usually light.

First Street has two options for cyclists. One is a dedicated bike lane on the road next to the curb—although it's only available about half of the time. The other is a combination bike-pedestrian trail on the east side of the road. If you can imagine a triple-wide sidewalk, then you'll have an image of what this trail looks like. Though this sidewalk/trail isn't the best option for road cyclists, it's great for casual bike riders who like to cruise along at a leisurely pace or for roller-bladers, runners or couples pushing strollers.

> "I was uncomfortable being on the road until I decided that I belonged there."

The 10% of First Street that does experience heavy traffic is near the intersection of 40th Avenue, where the street is four-lane for cars with no bike lane. Depending on time of day and traffic, I'll ride on the street *if* I feel I can move quickly through the intersection. When I do, I ride as fast as possible to flow with the traffic, but I sometimes switch to the sidewalk/trail to avoid congestion and get through the intersection safely.

On one ride, I had switched over to the sidewalk/trail since traffic was fairly heavy. I happened to notice a lady on a cruiser—a casual, single-speed bike—with a basket on the front handlebars, riding on the street in the lane closest to the curb. She was unhurried, cruising along at five miles per hour and seemingly oblivious to the fact that automobile traffic was stacking up behind her.

I could sense the cussing from a distance. Cars started honking, which brought no response from her. The traffic behind her started scrambling, furiously changing lanes to get around her and send her "messages" as they passed by. She cruised along, content in her own little world. She's fortunate she didn't cause an accident (or become one herself).

> "When one person knows what to expect from the other, things usually flow without issue. When they don't, things get more complicated."

Riding on the street was one of the biggest transitions I experienced when I began biking. Being around cars made me feel exposed and vulnerable. I was nervous about what to do when I encountered cars on the road.

And for good reason—bicycles are unique moving vehicles. Their top speed is slower than a car; they're smaller, and they aren't as visible. And, obviously, they don't have nearly the same safety features. In many ways, you feel intimidated. It's easy to feel like you get in the way, like you're a burden to other drivers.

As odd as this may sound, I was uncomfortable being on the road until I decided that I belonged there. Though I wasn't as big or fast as a car, I had to look in the mirror (so to speak) and convince myself it was okay for me to be on the road. I had to believe it. Once I did, I reached a comfort level with riding in and around cars.

I've learned that the motorist-cyclist encounter is not really that much different from when a motorist encounters any other vehicle on the road: When one person knows what to expect from the other, things usually flow without issue. When they don't, things get more complicated.

There are lots of little things a cyclist can and should do—like obeying all the traffic laws—but it comes down to this: When you're on the street, you have to act like a car. Motorists (usually) know what to expect from other motorists. Sometimes they just don't know what to expect from someone riding a bike.

Things work more smoothly when you act like the moving vehicle you are. You have to flow with traffic, not against it. You deserve the same rights as cars—nothing more, nothing less. You shouldn't expect any special treatment that is not typically given to other vehicles. Trouble comes when you believe you deserve special accommodation or act as if the road is yours and others should yield to you—same as if you were driving a car. You take the right of way when it's yours and give it when it's not. You should ride cautiously and defensively: Trust others, but allow for the reality that they may make a mistake.

> "If you're the leader, don't talk about being the leader. Just lead."

In many senses, leadership works the same way. You have to act like you belong as a leader, and you can't act like it unless you believe it.

I see this primarily for young or newly-promoted leaders who've not been in a position of influence before. It often comes up when newly promoted leaders have to direct a group of people who were previously peers. If this is you, then you'll need to deal with the awkwardness.

Where you previously gave input or opinion, now you have to give direction. It can be a gigantic leap for some new leaders to take. But you'll never be comfortable until you take it—and neither will your team.

You'll probably face the reality that some people don't want you there. They may resent the fact that you are the leader and will go so far as to try to make things uncomfortable for you. But this happens to seasoned and experienced leaders, too. This comes with the leadership territory, and you have to accept it and learn to manage it.

There's a leadership quality that goes beyond things like tenure, intelligence, strength, money or power. It's often referred to as having the moral authority to lead. When you're in the role and operating as a leader should, it's right for you to have influence over others. There's nothing wrong with it; it's morally acceptable.

I liken this situation to horseback riding. When the rider has assumed the moral authority to lead, the horse senses it and is comfortable and accepts the rider. If the rider has not assumed this role, the horse becomes uneasy and reluctant, and it will not be a good day for either horse or rider.

> "People (by and large) *want* to be led well. They may challenge their leader, but at the end of the day, people will respond to qualified, effective leadership."

One time I worked for a man who regularly reminded everyone he was in charge. "Someone has to be the leader," he would say, "And that person is me." After a while, I began to wonder if he actually believed what he was saying. No one else challenged or questioned that he was in a leadership role. Many, however, questioned his effectiveness.

Identifying yourself as the leader is necessary (see Chapter 6 – Being Invisible Will Get You Killed). But communicating repeatedly—"I'm in charge" or "I make the rules"—doesn't support your moral authority in the eyes of those you influence. It only makes them wonder if you're trying to convince yourself.

If you're the leader, don't talk about being the leader. Just lead. Don't gripe about the challenges of managing others. Just manage. Leadership requires courage; so stand up, dig deep and do what needs to be done.

People *need* to be led. People (by and large) *want* to be led well. They may challenge their leader, but at the end of the day, people will respond to qualified, effective leadership. Assuming you have the qualifications for the role, embrace the opportunity and lead. Then act like the leader people expect and need.

Put It in Motion

- **You Have to Act Like You Belong.** And in order to act like you belong as the leader, you have to believe that taking on the leadership role is the right thing.

- **Embrace the Moral Authority to Lead.** It's right to have influence on others. When you're in the role and operating as a leader should, then lead with confidence and a clear conscience.

- **Don't Talk About Leading, Just Lead.** It may be therapeutic for you, but discussing your leadership challenges with those you lead will often backfire on you. Instead, find a coach, a mentor or a trusted colleague if you need to vent, get perspective or think through options/ideas.

- **People Want to Be Well-Led.** People will respond to effective leadership.

6 – BEING INVISIBLE WILL GET YOU KILLED

"The visible signs of artful leadership are expressed, ultimately, in its practice."
Max DePree

It's happened more times than I'd like to admit: Close encounters of the vehicular kind.

I've had cars pulling out from a side street nearly hit me. And multiple times cars coming at me from the opposite direction have made a left turn right in front of me, causing me to take emergency evasive action.

A car pulling out on you is an ever-present reality you think about without trying to think about too much. The most common cause for these encounters is when motorists don't see bicycles. Sometimes this is obvious—like driving at night when it's hard to see anything that's not illuminated or at dusk or dawn when everything looks grey. Most of the time, however, motorists don't see cyclists because they simply aren't looking for them.

> "If you want to be an effective leader, others must see a leader when they look at you."

I've heard the same thing from motorcycle riders. Motorists develop the lazy habit of looking for other cars. And though they look right at you, they can't see you—because you're not a car. When this occurs, you become invisible; you just blend into the surroundings.

Knowing this as a cyclist is powerful knowledge. In addition to obvious steps to make yourself more visible—using a flashing headlamp, wearing a brightly-colored jersey or reflective straps on your ankles—I now work under the assumption that the motorists around me don't see me. I have become proactive.

31

For instance, when I see an oncoming car slow down and edge over—the behavior that indicates they are preparing to make a turn—I alter my behavior by sitting up in the saddle, raising my hand, etc. so the driver will see extra movement and realize I'm there.

I've also learned to discern where the motorist is looking. If their eyes are pointed at me for an extended time, chances are they've seen me. But if they glance my way and quickly turn their attention on to something else, there's a good chance I'm invisible. This is when the warning bells start going off in my head. I whistle loudly (I've got a pretty shrill whistle) and make plans to stop or get out of their way.

It's no coincidence that the frequency of these encounters has dropped significantly the longer I've been riding. This isn't because the motorist population has become more aware of cyclists on the road. It's because I've changed my behavior.

Because as a cyclist, it's essential that others see you.

> "People can't read your mind ... They can only respond to what they see in your behavior."

Visibility is also essential in leadership. If you want to be an effective leader, others must see a leader when they look at you. If your team doesn't "see you" as a leader—even though they may look right at you—they will continue on their path. You won't influence them, and they'll run over you in the process.

It's as simple as that.

Visibility is one of the most often overlooked aspects of leadership. At its core, leadership is an exhibited behavior. People can't read your mind. They don't know what you're thinking. They don't know your intentions or what you're feeling. They can only respond to what they see in your behavior: Your reactions (and whether they are over or underreactions), your tone of voice, your attitude, your consistency, your convictions and passion (or lack thereof), your focus, your patterns of thought, your communication tendencies ... they all create a leadership image that others interpret and then choose to follow (or not).

But my experience shows that so many leaders miss this reality. As a leader, you're on stage, and everyone's watching the performance. You're always on, from the moment you walk in the door until the moment you leave. Every action you take is visible and is open to evaluation.

This may sound unfair and even overwhelming. But, in fact, it is an opportunity: You get to determine what they see. I'm not suggesting you script every step. I am, however, suggesting you become aware of how you're behaving and become proactive in your approach to encounters with others.

Start by asking yourself, "I wonder what people see when they look at me..."

> "This may sound unfair and even overwhelming. But, in fact, it is an opportunity: You get to determine what they see."

It was one of the best days of my life.

My wife had thrown a surprise birthday party for me. The house was filled with friends, some of whom didn't know each other very well. I usually don't like being the center of attention, but this day was truly fun because everyone was genuinely enjoying the evening.

Later, I was looking at pictures of the event. One shot in particular stood out to me. Several of my friends, smiling and enjoying themselves, had posed for the picture.

I was in the photo, too, though I wasn't looking at the camera. I was in the background, obviously the listener in a one-on-one conversation. But the look on my face struck me. On one of the happiest days of my life, my face was saying it was one of the worst.

I'm typically optimistic, and I get energized being with others. But there's no way you'd know that by looking at my face. I looked sour, even angry. At that moment my face communicated impatience, disagreement and tension. And this was when I was having a great time. It scared me to think about what my face said on a bad day!

If you want to be more effective as a leader, you must become aware of what others see in your behavior. I can almost guarantee you there is something about your current behavior that is undercutting your level of influence—particularly if you aren't practicing self-awareness. Think about what others see when you complain, gripe, whine, overreact or lose your patience.

Remember, every conversation is an opportunity to shape your leadership, to apply laser focus to your influence. This is critical when you consider that opportunities to influence others are limited, and perceptions—once established—are not easily changed.

> "I can almost guarantee you there is something about your current behavior that is undercutting your level of influence."

If you've never thought about this, it may seem artificial—like you're acting or pretending to be somebody you're not. You may feel this is excessive, nonessential and that you can't afford the time and energy to devote to something that seems so ... superfluous.

I assure you nothing could be further from the truth. Seasoned leaders get it. They have developed the habit of recognizing opportunities when they present themselves and seizing them by managing their behavior accordingly. It is second nature for them. Taking control over what others see in your behavior may feel strange at first, but eventually you'll get comfortable with it.

Every chapter in this book touches on a leadership principle that at some point will be expressed in a behavior. These principles are not just things to *know*, they are things to *live*. It's not enough to know—intellectually—that they're relevant. They become effective *only* when they take up residence in your visible behavior.

Ultimately, it's up to you. You *can* keep your current behavior. But you'll have to deal with the consequences, which more than likely will result with you being in a reactive, defensive position.

If you want to influence people, they must be able to see you as an effective leader.

Put It in Motion

- **You Want Others to See You as a Leader.** Don't be overly concerned about being accepted, blending in or being "one of the gang"—not that these are wrong. They're just not nearly as important as being a good leader.

- **Leadership is a Behavior.** People can't read your mind. They can only respond to what they see. So make sure what they see is what you want them to see.

- **You're Always "On."** Your leadership (or lack thereof) is always on display—from the moment you walk in the door to the moment you leave.

- **Become Self-Aware.** I can almost guarantee you there is something about your current behavior that is undercutting your level of influence. Find out what it is, change it and then start looking for what to change next.

- **Leadership Is Not Something You *Know*, It's Something You *Do*.** Practice it. Live it out. Don't just think about it. Do it.

7 – THE START IS NOT THE FINISH

"The world is round and the place which may
seem like the end may also be only the beginning."
Ivy Baker Priest

The start of a ride is often my favorite part. The prep (the warm-up, stretching, pumping the tires, filling the water bottles, etc.) is done. Concerns and stressors are left behind. You clip into your pedals and settle onto the saddle. You are fresh. After the first few minutes of getting your heart rate up and establishing a rhythm, you feel like you could ride all day.

It's a wonderful feeling, one I wish I could bottle and sell. But it's gotten me into trouble more than once. For one, it's naïve: I can't ride all day. But even more damaging than this is the reality that performance at the beginning of the ride is rarely a good barometer of performance at the finish. I've had rides where I felt like a world beater at the start but felt just plain beat up at the end. I've had other rides where I felt like turning around after the warm-up stage, but pushing on resulted in some of my best rides ever.

> "...performance at the beginning of the ride is rarely a good barometer of performance at the finish."

In that sense, cycling is more of a marathon than a sprint. You go through distinct phases, each with its own characteristics, challenges and rewards. You can literally feel your body changing as the ride progresses and your hydration and nutrition levels ebb and flow. While these phases are somewhat predictable, each ride is unique. It requires continual awareness and intuition.

Leadership is seasonal as well. Challenges crop up. Moods change. People get distracted. Things shift unexpectedly and obstacles appear out of nowhere. The experiences of one phase are rarely an accurate barometer of how things will be in the next. So while leadership principles are constant, their application is not.

And more personally, your leadership conditioning will change as time in the role goes by. Early success—while a plus—is rarely a promise of success in later phases. And early struggles don't necessarily predict how you'll be doing once you've worked through them. So do the work and find your rhythm.

A group of people (a team, department, company, family, community, etc.) is a living organism which changes as it goes through time. The leader must sense the changes and have a finger on the pulse of the group as it goes about its business. Each season of its existence must be managed in its own time.

> "A group of people … is a living organism which changes as it goes through time."

Think of it this way: As an airliner progresses through a flight, things are constantly changing. The plane is burning off fuel, which changes the flight characteristics. The winds shift. The weather changes. New traffic comes into the airplane's flight space unpredictably. While the overall plan of arriving at the destination remains constant, the pilot must be aware of the changing circumstances and shifting environment and re-trim the aircraft so it flies efficiently, maintains the flight plan and arrives safely at the scheduled time.

All of this requires a leader to have a sense of presence: An awareness of the situation and circumstances, and the ability to act appropriately to the current conditions. That's why communication is one of the most important tools in your toolbox. Asking questions of your team and actively listening to their responses will allow you to gain insight into what's really going on.

- Are people telling you what you want to hear or what you need to hear?
- Do they really know what to do, or are they figuring it out on the fly?

- Are the tasks clear, objectively measurable and attainable?

Look for behavioral clues that the team is prepared not just to do the task in front of them but to anticipate problems and seize opportunities.
- Are people working together or against each other? Are the separate initiatives aligned?
- Do people have the resources they need?
- Are they coming back to you for information or criteria or decisions they could—or should—have made themselves?
- Said another way—have you worked your way into a micro-management pattern without realizing it?

These are the types of things that derail novice leaders. They haven't learned the wisdom that comes from experience. Mature, effective leaders have learned the ability to look beyond the obvious and immediate to recognize "seasons" their organization experiences.

This often looks like intuition or some kind of sixth sense. But it's actually not that mysterious. It comes from a disciplined intent to adjust and adapt accordingly—

"This often looks like intuition, or some kind of sixth sense. But it's actually not that mysterious."

often before the new environment presents itself. Practiced leaders have learned (usually through painful experience and failure) that using the dynamics and outcomes of one season of an organization's existence to predict another can get you into trouble and will blind you to both obstacles and opportunities.

You can't let how you feel in one phase determine how you're going to approach other phases. You can't predict how the ride as a whole is going to shape out—each part of the ride must be managed separately and in its own time.

Put It in Motion

- **Leadership Principles Are Constant, But Their Application is Not.** Things and people shift constantly. Don't expect that what worked once will work the same way next time.

- **Your Leadership Condition Will Change Over Time.** Early success is rarely a predictor of success in later phases.

- **A Group of People is a Living Organism.** Expect that their attitudes and performance will ebb and flow. Keep your finger on the pulse of your team to know what state they're in and how best to lead them *today*.

- **Ask Lots of Questions and Then Listen Closely.** This is one of the best ways to look beyond the obvious and immediate to find out what state your team is in.

---

8 – HUMILITY

*"Humility leads to strength and not to weakness.
It is the highest form of self-respect to admit mistakes
and to make amends for them."*
John J. McCloy

Peter Demens (originally Petrovitch Demenschev) was an exiled Russian nobleman, who emigrated to the U.S. and settled in Florida in May of 1881. Demens went to work in a sawmill in Central Florida. In short order, he bought out the owners and built the company into one of the largest contractors in Florida at that time. When the Orange Belt Railway couldn't pay him for his work a few years later, he got into the railroad business and took over ownership.

The prospect of prosperity and New York funding enticed him to push the narrow gauge rail line from the Orlando area to the Gulf of Mexico. On May 1, 1888, the line was completed to its terminus—a remote, unnamed outpost with no real streets. Demens named the area after the city of his youth, St. Petersburg.

> "...it's not about where you start; it's about where you want to finish."

Progress and development eventually made the line obsolete. But abandoned rail lines often make for good biking trails, and in the 1980's the right of way was purchased by Pinellas County, paved and reborn as the Fred Marquis Pinellas Trail. It's now a 40-mile biking and hiking trail that stretches from Demens Landing in downtown St. Pete north to Tarpon Springs. It has proven to be a convenient testing ground for many a new cyclist.

I remember my first extended ride on the trail as a novice. At 30 miles, it was twice as far as I'd previously ridden, making it a challenge. I was keeping up what I thought was a good pace and feeling pretty good about it. Then, on my return leg, everything changed. I was second-guessing this whole idea of biking for exercise. My butt hurt, my legs hurt, my neck hurt. Stopping just prolonged the torture. The only thing to do was to keep going.

Struggling to maintain a rhythm, I found myself at one of the bridge crossings, which made my struggles even more apparent. As I was switching to a lower gear to make it up the ramp, two riders passed me. One was a petite woman, not much over five feet tall and not much heavier than 100 pounds. The other was a guy with big calf muscles.

"How you doin' buddy?" he said as they passed.

> "...we all need the right mirror to see ourselves accurately."

I can't remember what response tumbled out of my mouth, but it didn't matter anyway; they were quickly out of earshot.

It was, shall we say, a reorientation. When riders pass you, going uphill, smiling and talking to each other, you know something about yourself you didn't moments earlier. You know where you stand; you know who you really are.

It wasn't as demoralizing as it sounds. I'd been riding for a while that day, and for all I knew, they had just started (okay, that's probably grasping at straws). I was struggling at that point but was soon able to push through it and get my wind back. The long and short of it is that I was a rookie still trying to find my legs. I was making progress. It was a sobering and encouraging reminder that by staying with the process of growth I will be stronger.

I will change.

Looking back on it—where 30 miles is now a maintenance ride—I'm a completely different person. I feel both strangely satisfied and hungry to grow more. I've made progress. Yet realize I have much further to go than I first thought.

After all, it's not about where you start; it's about where you want to finish.

It's been said that we all need the right mirror to see ourselves accurately. This is especially true for leaders. You'd think it would be obvious, yet experience tells me genuine humility is a rare leadership quality. Many leaders don't take the time to look in the mirror—or when they do, they use a mirror that doesn't give them a true image.

It's part of the leader's job to help others see things as they really are, to build a common clarity and perspective on reality. Leaders who can't—or more disappointingly won't—see themselves accurately discredit themselves because people won't trust a leader who can't see what everyone else can.

> "Leaders who can't—or more disappointingly won't—see themselves accurately discredit themselves because people won't trust a leader who can't see what everyone else can."

Another part of the leader's job is to help those they lead to improve and develop themselves. But if leaders have no interest in developing and growing themselves, how will they have the skills to help others develop? If they can't see themselves accurately enough to know how and where to grow, how effective can they truly be? It's hypocritical; leaders shouldn't have an expectation for their people that they don't also have for themselves.

It's good to be reoriented: to break out of your routine enough to see yourself as you really are—and to be comfortable with that. It's good to know both your *capabilities* as well as your *liabilities*, to taste the fruit of change without the bitterness of guilt and failure over not being good enough. It brings balance to life. It liberates the ego from the hard toil of convincing yourself (and others) of a false self-worth.

When I'm more focused on who I can be tomorrow, I'm less focused on trying to validate who I am today.

It's good to be humble(d).

Put It in Motion

- **Humility Is a Well-Respected—But Rare—Leadership Trait.** Why is that? Here's a coaching question: What, if anything, is preventing it in you?

- **Leaders Need a Mirror to See Themselves Accurately.** Only then can they begin to move toward genuine humility. Do what you can to get a true picture of yourself.

- **Leaders Help to Clearly Define Reality.** Your team's response to their situation depends (in part) on how you characterize it.

- **People Won't Trust Leaders Who Can't See Their Own Developmental Needs.** If a leader can't see himself/herself clearly, why would anyone else trust that leader's feedback about how to improve leadership effectiveness?

- **Set a High Bar for Your Leadership and Keep Striving for It.** When we're more focused on who we can be tomorrow, we're less focused on validating who we are today.

9 – BY THE SWEAT OF YOUR BROW

"Nothing will work unless you do."
Maya Angelou

A road bike has a lot of gear combinations; mine has 30. With all those gearing options, you might be tempted to think it would take all the work out of cycling. Not so.

Riding a bike brings the inescapable realization (often indicated by the sweat dripping into your eyes) that you are a self-propelled mechanism. Being self-propelled means two things. First, any movement forward requires work to be performed. Second, *you* generate that work. There are occasions when you get to coast downhill (which required you first to give double effort to get up the hill), but most of the time, you're what's moving you. This work requires a certain level of commitment and preparation, which is where the line separating serious and casual cycling begins.

Work is a physics unit of measure (expressed in units called joules). It's the force applied to an object multiplied by the distance the object moves. In cycling, the limits of your ability to produce work get exposed quickly.

> "…any movement forward requires work to be performed."

Beyond the obvious step of developing more leg strength and better cardio capacity, there are two areas that affect the level of work: efficiency and weight.

Efficiency

In cycling, the work performed is equivalent to the force you apply to the pedals multiplied by the distance the bike travels. The more effectively this force is applied, the more work that gets produced.

There are many ways that work effort can be lost. One is having flexible equipment. When you push down on the pedals, for instance, you don't want your shoes flexing and absorbing energy that would otherwise be transferred to the pedals. That's why biking shoes have incredibly stiff soles. The goal of bicycle design is to make the critical components as stiff as possible.

Energy can also be lost in the pedaling motion. When your knees are moving side-to-side, additional energy is lost (to say nothing of the damage done to the knee). The same applies for moving your upper body side-to-side, which will never translate force into the pedals. This is all wasted energy.

When you watch head-on television coverage of professional cyclists, watch their upper bodies and their knees: You'll see virtually no side-to-side motion in the pedal strokes. They're still in the saddle. Their legs go straight up, then straight down—even when they are laboring to get up a hill. Millions of pedal strokes have proven that the smart way to increase work is to avoid any extraneous leg movement.

"...you have to find your own inefficiencies and eliminate them."

This may sound extreme, but on a bike you quickly discover that details like these make your work easier and yield more output.

When it comes to the work of a leader, attention to efficiency is paramount. There are so many ways to expend energy yet not increase work output. They're too numerous to list and too individual to be universally applied. Meaning—you have to find your own inefficiencies and eliminate them. But look for them; when you do, you'll find them.

If you're not sure where to begin, try taking stock of the way you manage your calendar. Are you trying to do creative efforts at the end of the day, when you're fatigued and distracted?

How about your priorities: Are you spending too much time on things that can—and should—be delegated? Are you spending energy working on urgent issues instead of important issues? Are you working on stuff you *like* to do or stuff you *should* do?

Or look at your communication patterns. Can you give direction and cast vision with more clarity and focus? More consistency?

How about diversifying how you plan and manage your work? Are you trying to solve problems using the same old approaches? Remember Einstein's quote: "We cannot solve our problems with the same thinking we used when we created them."

How about broadening your ability to work? Are you involving your team in coming up with creative solutions (which means you have to invite, incent and reward them)? Are there other things consuming your time and energy (like, I don't know, email perhaps)?

> "We cannot solve our problems with the same thinking we used when we created them."
>
> *Albert Einstein*

Weight

When it comes to weight, less is most definitely more.

In cycling you're pedaling to move your own weight, the weight of the bike and everything you're carrying (feel free to add, "Well, duh"). But as obvious as it might be, you'd be surprised at how much of a revelation this is to new cyclists. The less you take with you the better.

Some cyclists are obsessive about weight. In pro cycling, thousands of dollars are spent to shave mere ounces off the weight of the bike. I used to think this was fanatically overzealous until I started pedaling my own weight around. While I don't have their budget, I do share the desire to be as minimalist as I can be when it comes to extra load.

Of course, you must take fluids and nutrition. You have to bring things you hope you never have to use like an extra tube in case you get a flat. But if it doesn't serve a purpose for the ride, don't bring it along. Extra stuff just means more work, with less progress.

There are numerous things that weigh down a team or an organization. The biggest of these is people who don't contribute as teammates. I've seen whole teams affected by one person who isn't on board, doesn't get it, has toxic interpersonal behaviors or isn't committed to the team's purpose and goals.

Sometimes a team member's "weight" comes from things like skill level, experience or capacity (their ability to think at a level that's necessary for the job role). Most of the time, though, the determining factor for weightiness centers on attitude. You can train to increase skills; you can't do much with a bad attitude. People who are coachable, who are looking for a way to contribute to something beyond their own self-interest and who want to be part of a team will conform and accept a role on the team. Those who don't, won't.

> "I've seen whole teams affected by one person who isn't on board, doesn't get it, has toxic interpersonal behaviors or simply isn't committed to the team's purpose and goals."

It's not always about people though. Sometimes it's things like a history of failure or debt. Sometimes it's a bad reputation.

Sometimes it's a blind spot that you just can't put your finger on. You may have a sense that something's lurking, weighing you and your team down. If so, a great resource (though a bit dated) is *The Thing in the Bushes: Turning Organizational Blind Spots into Competitive Advantage*. The title alone gives you an idea of the book's value: It helps you see the hidden things that distract, delay and handcuff your organization's weighty baggage.

The responsibility of the leader is to make sure the organization is moving forward, predictably and effectively. You can do that by being more efficient and getting rid of the things that weigh on your team, your processes and yourself.

There are occasions when you get to coast, but they usually come only when you've given double the effort to get over a challenge. The work of the leader requires a certain level of commitment and preparation, which is where the line separating excellence and mediocrity often begins.

Put It in Motion

- **There Are Many Ways to Expend Energy That Don't Result in Increased Work Output.** You have to find your own inefficiencies and eliminate them. Look for them in your calendar, your priorities, your communication patterns, your planning and management approaches, your methods of analysis (or over-analysis); when you do, you'll find them.

- **People Who Aren't With You Are Extra Weight.** That doesn't mean they're bad people, but it does mean they're a bad fit. Think long and hard about this before bringing them on your team, and probe to determine their attitude and values to make sure they're a good match for your organization.

10 – FORWARD THINKING

"Create your future from your future,
not your past."
Werner Erhard

Bicycles are amazing machines to move you forward. Backing up, however, is another story.

One day, at the end of a ride, I stopped at the gate going into my community. A car, obviously a visitor, was at the keypad trying unsuccessfully to call their party to open the gate. The keypad is to the right of the gate on a separate circle driveway to prevent visitors from impeding traffic.

Just as I came to a stop, a resident drove up behind me and clicked their remote to open the gate. This put me between the visitor to my right (who obviously wanted to seize the opportunity of an open gate) and the resident behind me who was making motions to get around me.

> "Many parts of the human experience compel us to move backward ... there are so many reasons to look for ways to circle the wagons—if not retreat altogether."

I decided to ease back out of the way and let them both pass, which involved walking my bike backwards. Standing over my bike and trying to be quick about it, I began taking short, shuffle steps as I looked backward to steer off to the side and avoid the cars. My reverse action was also aided by the ground that sloped away from the gate. The decline sped my descent and things quickly became awkward.

I lengthened my stride to keep pace with my backward momentum. Just about the time I had it under control, my left pedal made contact with my shin. Everything came to an immediate, painful stop. Fortunately I stayed upright, and I had backed up far enough for both cars to pass. But the bruise on my shin served as a painful reminder: Bikes and their riders are made to go forward not backward.

As I mentioned in the Introduction, living with a forward-facing attitude is a deeply personal conviction. So much so that I had it painted on my bike in Latin—*Semper Incito*: Always Forward. Perhaps more than any other, this one principle captures everything I discuss about leadership.

> "This rearward tendency is why we need leaders to skillfully and artfully help us dream, hope, pick ourselves up when we stumble and animate success from failure."

Semper Incito is the essence behind one of the five practices of exemplary leadership in the classic *Leadership Challenge* by Jim Kouzes and Barry Posner: Inspiring a Shared Vision. It's a quality of leaders to envision a desired future; and this future state is so compelling, real and attainable that it can't *not* be pursued.

Many parts of the human experience compel us to move backward. Fear, guilt, regret, lack of reconciliation with others (or ourselves) ... there are so many reasons to look for ways to circle the wagons—if not retreat altogether. They affect us at almost every level: socially, emotionally, practically, spiritually, organizationally and more. Like gravity, they relentlessly pull us toward focusing on reasons to fail, to give up, to entrench, to blame and find fault, to avoid risk and to wrap ourselves in blankets of safety.

This rearward tendency is why we need leaders to skillfully and artfully help us dream, hope, pick ourselves up when we stumble and animate success from failure. We need leaders with their feet planted tangibly in the here and now but with hearts and imaginations playing downstream—in the potential and uncertainty of the horizon. It's one of the most elusive of leadership qualities, and it does not come easily or conveniently. It's forged, cultivated.

And I've never seen an effective, accomplished leader who navigated in reverse.

Not one.

There are four basic applications of the principle of forward thinking:
1. Initiate
2. Drive for results
3. Leverage success (Chapter 19 – Presume Nothing)
4. Learn from failure (Chapter 22 – The Wall is Real, and Hitting it Hurts)

Leaders take initiative. Aptly put by Bill Hybels, "Leaders have a bias for action." They get started, and then start things. They don't wait (unless waiting is what needs to be done). They call people out. They talk about the elephant in room—the obvious issues others are avoiding. They're proactive. They're the spark.

"I have never seen an effective, accomplished leader who navigated in reverse."

Driving for results comes after initiating and is one of the most recognizable traits of a leader. Leaders push forward when others simply will not. They're driven, almost relentlessly. They're impatient with ambiguity. They seek closure and accomplishment. They have a focus on the target and don't get bogged down with distractions, setbacks or details.

Seasoned, skillful leaders take the drive for results and add to it the ability to both leverage success wisely and learn from failure so mistakes aren't repeated. Both of these sound obvious and easy to deploy but in practice are anything but. Many leaders stop at driving for results and miss the other two finer aspects of an always-forward orientation.

The goal is in front of you, and if it were easy, it'd be done by now. You can't operate off yesterday's results, good or bad. Yesterday's ride was yesterday. Today's ride is unique and has its own challenges and rewards. Today—and every day that follows—is an opportunity, one that must be seized to be realized. It must never be presumed upon or taken for granted. It must be faced with a mix of courage and caution, confidence and wisdom, excitement and realism.

If you want to have any measure of effectiveness as a leader, you must embrace moving forward with unapologetic bias.

Today, and each day after.

Put It in Motion

- **Many People Tend to Hold Onto the Present, If Not Live in the Past.** You would do well to remember that this is a natural human tendency. Fight the urge to hold it against people or think less of them because of it.

- **Make Your Hope Real.** Because of the point above, even a little bit of genuine hope goes a long way. Just make sure it's genuine. Avoid casting "hope" that comes across as cheap, conditional or accompanied by a hidden agenda.

- **You Can't Navigate in Reverse.** You can't lead effectively by reliving—or trying to overcome—the past. As the opening quote says, "You have to create your future from your future."

- **Try to Keep Four Things in Balance.**

  1) **Initiate** – Don't wait, pause or hold back; get things going.

  2) **Drive for Results** – Keep pushing forward and don't get stalled by indecision or over-analysis.

  3) **Leverage Success** – Find what works and repeat it.

  4) **Learn From Failure** – Learn what didn't work—and why—and don't repeat it.

11 – ATTITUDE AND EVERYTHING

"An adventure is only an inconvenience rightly considered.
An inconvenience is only an adventure wrongly considered."
G.K. *Chesterton*

I have to be honest.

There are days I don't want to ride. I just don't want to get up early. If the weather is sketchy on days like this, I'm convinced it's going to end up raining.

I catch myself feeling like I don't want to go through the effort to prepare, to eat right and wake up early. I don't feel like taking care of my gear, or cleaning or working on my bike to keep it in top shape.

Often, these days stretch into weeks. Since most of my riding is done on the weekends, if I go a weekend without getting in a serious ride, it sometimes stretches into two weeks. Before you know it, I've gone close to a month without riding productively. And if I miss that much time, when I *do* get serious again, I've lost my cardio shape. It's like starting all over again.

"...attitude isn't everything. But it affects everything."

Come to think of it, there are lots of other things I could do with the three to four hours I'd sit in the saddle.

I question whether riding is really doing me much good. In fact, part of me admits it's probably hurting me in the long run. I'll bet that 20 years from now my knees are going to be shot. They'll probably need to be replaced.

And think of the money I spend on bicycle tubes and nutrition and the electrolyte solution I put in my water bottles. I could have used it for entertainment or something else important.

What's the point of it all anyway?

So, let me ask you: How do you feel after reading the rant above? Want to keep reading? Do you want to go get on your bike?

Did reading the negative, whiny, I-give-up attitude make you want to invest more of yourself in your current priorities? Do you want to apply yourself to a greater degree: to sacrifice the additional time and effort it will take to move the needle—even a little bit—in whatever noble cause you are currently invested?

> "Your attitude is contagious, whether it is good or bad."

My guess is no.

If it affects you this way by reading it, think about how much greater the impact when you experience it live and in person? How does it affect you when you have to be around others who are griping, whining, complaining and being pessimistic about their circumstances?

Then ask yourself: I wonder what others see and hear in my behavior when I'm around them?

A Life Half-Full

When it comes to leadership, attitude isn't everything. Leadership is much more complex than that. If attitude was everything, this would be the only chapter in this book. No, attitude isn't everything. But it *affects* everything; it touches everything. Attitude shapes and colors and animates everything leaders do.

> "Leadership is the art of getting someone else to do something *you* want done because *he* wants to do it."
>
> *Dwight Eisenhower*

Effective leaders believe that it (whatever "it" is) can be done; in fact, they believe it *must* be done. But this *"must"* isn't a sense of forced compliance like a rule or a law. An effective, influential attitude views *"must"* as the right thing to do—as if "it" is something we can't not do.

Leadership promotes, inspires and changes the default attitudes people often have about an objective or a goal. Human nature is such that so many of us have a natural glass-half-empty bias. Your role as a leader is to make "it" important, relevant and vital enough that people believe "it" *must* be accomplished; that "it" *can* be and *will* be accomplished. Dwight Eisenhower said it well: "Leadership is the art of getting someone else to do something *you* want done because *he* wants to do it."

Contagion

Your attitude is contagious, whether it's good or bad.

The attitude you carry will usually be the attitude the team adopts. That's because (to borrow Max De Pree's words) leaders create the reality in which their teams operate. Attitude is like the atmosphere: Your team breathes it in. It can be toxic, depressing or heavy; it can be impossible. Or it can be fulfilling, challenging, rewarding and "do-able."

Leaders, most of the time, are more effective when they can remain positive even in the midst of setback, disappointment or challenge. When leaders can remain positive, it creates an upbeat, productive environment for their team. When leaders get pessimistic or stressed, it causes their team to have doubts about the future and begin to worry and stress themselves.

> "As a leader, you're always 'on stage.' Your team is always watching you whether they realize it or not."

That's probably not an earth-shattering piece of news, but here's the reality you must face: As a leader, you can't effectively project optimism, vision and stability if you're not in the right frame of mind. In other words, you can't fake it—your team will see right through it if you try. Which means your best chance of *appearing* positive to your team is for you to genuinely *be* positive.

You may dismiss this as simply feel-good, sunshine-pumped salesmanship, but it is scientifically supported. In 1998 Dr. Martin Seligman founded the Positive Psychology Center at the University of Pennsylvania in Philadelphia. In contrast with clinical psychology, which focuses on emotional *dis*-ease, positive psychology focuses on emotional *ease*. It looks at the environments and dynamics that allow humans to operate effectively, productively and from a position of engagement. It identifies ways people obtain a higher level of connection with their work and with others. When people are not "at ease," they are uncomfortable. They tend to withdraw, pull back, take fewer risks and become skeptical; they demonstrate a lack of trust.

Creating a consistently positive environment is one of the most profound things you can do as a leader to increase the level of influence you have on others. Because genuinely positive team environments are so rare in our society today, people are hungry to find them. And once they've experienced it, they engage and commit at levels other teams can only dream of.

As a leader, you're always "on stage" (see Chapter 6 – Being Invisible Will Get You Killed). Your team is always watching you whether they realize it or not. So you must get ready before you walk in the door.

> "Never underestimate the power that exists in your words and thoughts as a leader and their effect on your team—and yourself."

Challenge yourself to think about the day from a positive point of view. When you approach the day with positive attitudes, it adds energy, a sense of urgency and a belief that things can get done. People in influential positions can drastically affect an outcome—often unintentionally—based on the attitudes they present.

The words and thoughts of a leader are powerful and can operate as self-fulfilling prophecies. Leaders can pre-determine an outcome that their teams will then produce. If you believe things will go badly, often times they will. If you believe a solution is out there waiting to be discovered, many times you will find it. You can make it hard, depressing or hopeless. Or conversely you can make it productive, fun or rewarding—just in the way you frame it.

Of course, having the right state of mind isn't a silver bullet or cure-all. It's only one element in the leadership toolkit. But it's powerful, when used effectively.

Hal Moore is a retired U.S. Army lieutenant general who is best known for leading his unit in the 1965 Battle of Ia Drang, portrayed by Mel Gibson in the movie *We Were Soldiers Once*. One of his most notable leadership traits is the belief that there is always one more thing you can do. There's another avenue, another solution, a work-around, a way out, over or through. You just have to find it. Moore credits this attitude, which his men had come to believe, as one of the reasons the unit survived and won the brutal two-day battle.

Never underestimate the power that exists in your words and thoughts as a leader and their effect on your team—and yourself.

Put It in Motion

- **Your Attitude—Both Good and Bad—is Contagious.** Be what you want to reproduce in others. Be the living example of what you want those around you to be.

- **Attitude Affects Everything.** A bad attitude saps inspiration, invites criticism, deflates motivation, erodes trust and reduces engagement. A good attitude increases all of the above.

- **Make it Genuine.** This is more than just being Captain Encouragement. You can't just *act* positive. You have to genuinely *be* positive. If you're not, people will see it as an act.

- **Attitude Can Be Self-Fulfilling.** Your influence affects the outcome (duh!). That's why it's called leadership. In that regard, attitude works just like planning or strategy.

- **Your Thoughts and Your Words Are Powerful.** You can impact someone's day; you might impact someone's life.

- **There's Always One More Thing You Can Do.** First, believe it's there. Second, go find it.

12 – KEEP YOUR MOUTH SHUT...

"Man does not live by words alone,
despite the fact that sometimes he has to eat them."
Adlai Stevenson

When we first moved to Florida, we were told there were two kinds of homes: Those that *have* termites and those that *will* have termites. Central Florida's subtropical temperature zone is like a nature preserve for bugs: They thrive here.

Some of these bugs are of the flying variety. And they are not immune from flying around bike trails, especially after a rain. For some reason that I'm guessing has something to do with either eating or procreation, the bugs are out in force after a rain.

I sometimes come back from a ride pelted with gnats. Of course, you never see them; you feel them hitting your body, smearing your sunglasses and collecting on your arms.

I've gotten to the point where I can almost predict when I'm about to ride into a gnat cloud—a dip in the road or perhaps a spot shielded from the wind and near a still body of water. It's like a sixth sense that gives me the warning ahead of time.

> "...at some point you'll encounter bugs. So you learn when to keep your mouth closed. Otherwise you'll eat something you hadn't planned on."

Many times, but not every time.

If you cycle in Florida, at some point you'll encounter bugs. So you learn pretty quickly when to keep your mouth closed. Otherwise, you'll eat something you hadn't planned on—and usually it's pretty (g)nasty.

61

There's another leadership principle that works the same way, though it's not to protect you from what might go in your mouth. It's to protect you from what might come out of it. Communication is a vital leadership tool. As it relates to what comes out of your mouth, you'll probably talk more in a leadership role than you will in other roles. You'll find yourself giving your input on things—whether it's solicited or not. Leaders encourage, comment, challenge, prod, instruct, correct, reprove, confide, share and comfort more than almost any other role in an organization.

Doing those things well is a challenge. Doing them with excellence—consistently, through all kinds of situations and scenarios—is special. This is what leaders must do if they hope to achieve influence.

> "Leaders encourage, comment, challenge, prod, instruct, correct, reprove, confide, share and comfort more than almost any other role in an organization."

You'll be tempted to say things you probably shouldn't. You'll have opportunity to say what's on your mind. You'll react to events with unfiltered judgment or commentary.

You'll do well if you learn when to keep your mouth shut. Otherwise, you'll have to eat the words that come out—and sometimes they can be nasty.

You'll be tempted to talk about other people. Just remember—communication is a behavior. When you're talking about people who aren't in the room, the people who are in the room will, at some point, be convinced you also talk about them when they're not in the room. Is that what you want? How will that help establish your leadership credibility or your trustworthiness?

As I mentioned in Chapter 11 – Attitude and Everything, I love the perspective of Max De Pree when he says that leaders define reality for the people they lead. And they do this largely through their communication. They give context. They can turn challenges into a doomsday scenario or into the organization's finest hour—just by how they talk about them. Parents can stigmatize their children for life or instill an unbridled sense of self-worth and confidence—just by choosing their words carefully and saying them the right way.

Perhaps the most vital thing about what comes out of your mouth as a leader is this: Make it truthful.

Don't ever say anything that's not true.

Ever.

No, I mean it. Never. Not for any reason.

Not as a joke; not to make a point, close a sale or win an argument. Nothing is important enough—or irrelevant enough—to excuse intentionally saying something that's not true.

Think about how you handle the truth. Why would you ever want people to question whether they should believe what you say? Why would you, for instance, casually preface a statement by saying something like, "Now, I'm not going to lie to you..."

Really, now that's a relief.

When it comes to truth, there are no shades.

As I said earlier, leaders define reality for their team. Why would you want their reality skewed or in any way clouded?

The number one quality of a leader is trust. Without trust, you cannot lead—no matter what other competencies you bring to the table. If people can't trust you, they won't follow you.

It's that simple.

When it comes to trust, if there's a glimmer of doubt it's gone.

> "...leaders define reality for the people they lead. And they do this largely through their communication."

And, of course, the gnat illustration breaks down a bit when you consider that not all leadership communication issues revolve around over-communication or miscommunication. Sometimes, the issue is a lack of communication. You'll do yourself well to say more, not less, when it comes to encouragement. Give your people hope. When they do a good job, tell them so (but never do this when it was a poor job—that wouldn't be the truth).

The choice is yours. You're responsible for the words that come out of your mouth. I've yet to see a leader who couldn't improve on his or her communication skills. You'll never perfect it; it's life-long skill development. But you can dramatically increase your leadership leverage by practicing it.

Daily.

Put It in Motion

- **Communication is the Leader's Most Used Instrument.** It's either helping you, or it's hurting you. *Everything* you say as a leader either enhances or undermines your influence.

- **Most Leaders Are Unaware of Their Communication Tendencies.** If you choose to become aware of yours, you will be so much further ahead.

- **Remember, Communication is a Behavior.** People form opinions and respond to you based on what they see (and hear) in your communication.

- **It's Not Hard to Change, But You Have to at Least Try.** Communication can be modified. It's not hard, but because you're changing old habits you must be intentional and persistent to see real change.

- **Your Communication Defines Reality for Your Team.** How you talk about things shapes how others see it. Make it positive, when possible, and make it real.

- **Always be Truthful.** Don't ever tell anyone something that's not true. That doesn't mean you have to be forthcoming about everything; it just means that you never intentionally deceive.

- **Encouragement is Free, and Priceless.** Give it away, liberally, because people need it.

13 – ...AND KEEP YOUR EYES OPEN

"Opportunity is sometimes hard to recognize if you're only looking for a lucky break."
Monta Crane

Cycling has another inevitability: road hazards.

There are the obvious stationary hazards: rocks, sand, nails or screws, potholes, cracks or tree branches ... I never knew there was so much junk on the road until I started cycling.

Then there are the moving hazards: cars, people (especially kids), dogs, etc. This is where it gets, um ... interesting.

I've had cars cross the road right in front of me, apparently having never seen me (see Chapter 6 – Being Invisible Will Get You Killed). Presumably, they checked for oncoming cars (not bicycles) and, seeing none, hit the gas. If I hadn't performed an emergency stop, there would have been a nasty collision, and I would have come out on the losing end.

> **"Being on a bike has forced me to look further out, to develop the habit of anticipation and to see everything—not just the obvious."**

As strange as this may sound, I can deal with the cars. They are fairly predictable, and I've learned how to tell whether the driver has seen me. What I can't deal with are squirrels. They wait until you approach to bound onto the trail, sans purpose, and stop. Once in the open, they seem frozen in confusion, caught in the squirrel version of no-man's land. At the last instant, utter panic takes over, and they scramble in some direction that no one can anticipate. You have to wonder how a species that makes itself more vulnerable at the approach of danger hasn't gone extinct by now.

One time a squirrel stopped 80% of the way across the trail, moving from my right to my left. I countered by moving all the way to my right, giving him a wide berth. When I got close he jumped as if to complete the crossing. But then, inexplicably, he panicked and darted in front of me back to where he started from. By that time, I was on top of him. Miraculously, I missed him; though I still can't figure out how.

> "Failure to look ahead means last-second, abrupt and potentially dangerous evasive action—which oftentimes could have been avoided."

I've become sobered by the reality that road hazards can have a bigger impact on an exposed cyclist than on a motorist wearing a seat belt, surrounded by airbags. I guess this reality has changed how I see where I'm going. I see things ... differently; I look for things I never saw from the cocoon of an automobile. Being on a bike has forced me to look further out, to develop the habit of anticipation and to see everything—not just the obvious.

On a bike, it all happens in front.

This is also true for leaders: Most of what you need to watch for happens in front of you. It's up ahead. And as you approach it, you must be looking for it—because it likely won't be obvious, much less anticipated.

> "...it's not just hazards we miss by not looking out front: Opportunities can be missed just as easily."

This requires you to see things ... differently, to look further out; to anticipate. It requires seeing everything, not just the obvious. This almost always requires reflection to check your gut and challenge your assumptions. It requires a curiosity to look beyond the typical leadership metrics.

Looking out front can be difficult to do when you have so many demands upon your time, focus and energy. But the sooner you see the hazard, the better equipped you will be to adjust, adapt and steer around it.

Failure to look ahead means last-second, abrupt and potentially dangerous evasive action—which oftentimes could have been avoided.

Bear in mind that it's not just hazards we miss by not looking out front: Opportunities can be missed just as easily. The last thing you want to do is stumble across an opportunity without recognizing it or being prepared to seize it. And here's the good news: The same principles apply when it comes to looking for both hazards and opportunities.

It all happens in front.

Put It in Motion

- **It All Happens Out Front.** Look forward to shape your future, and look behind to gain wisdom.

- **Start Looking Further Out.** The sooner you see things coming, the better position you'll be in to adjust and adapt.

- **Learn to Look at Everything, Not Just the Obvious.** Stay objective and neutral, get out of your paradigm and get into the right mindset

- **What You Choose to Look at Matters.** You can look right at something and not see it. You can look at something and not recognize it for what it is.

- **What You Choose to See Matters.** Avoid selective blindness, and discipline yourself to see the whole picture. For example, don't get caught in the trap of seeing only the risks and missing the opportunities or seeing who people aren't and not seeing who they are.

---

14 – DECIDE—NOW

"Determine that the thing can and shall be done,
and then we shall find the way."
Abraham Lincoln

Most of the time, my rides are well-planned. I usually take one of several familiar routes, and I know how much fluid and nutrition to take along. I have route contingencies planned in case I want to cut the ride short or lengthen it if I feel up to it.

Yet with all the planning, I still have to deal with many unknowns. I've found that cycling is a decision-intensive experience. The environment is fluid, and circumstances are unique from one ride to the next—even when riding the same route at the same time of day.

> "In this fluid environment, what—and how— I decide may be inconsequential. Or it could be a matter of life and death."

- How do I best navigate through this intersection?
- How should I maneuver around that pedestrian traffic?
- What are the surface conditions on this corner?
- Should I pull in behind this other rider I've overtaken or pass them?
- Is that black spot just tar, or is it debris that could puncture my tire?
- I'm falling behind my pace: Why, and should I pick it up?

In this fluid environment, what—and how—I decide may be inconsequential. Or it could be a matter of life and death.

Making quality decisions is a trait I've found to be common in all good leaders. Part of this comes from practice; after all, decision-making is one of the main responsibilities of a leader. Because it comes with the territory, there are countless opportunities to work on decision-making.

Unless you decide not to.

By that I mean (like most areas of leadership) results are not automatic: Having the opportunity for practice and leveraging that practice for development are two entirely different things (see Chapter 16 – Practice Doesn't Make Perfect). Unfortunately, many people in positions of influence aren't quality decision-makers. So if you want to make better decisions, I'll give you six things to focus on.

Food for thought: Many of these traits may appear to contradict each other. What does that tell you about the nature of decision-making as a leadership competency?

"... there are countless opportunities to work on decision-making. Unless you decide not to."

Be Decisive

It's been said that the only thing worse than a wrong decision is no decision at all. It's not *always* true, but it's spot-on in most circumstances. Being decisive is about *making* the decision.

Decisions move things. Until decisions are made, people are waiting for direction; they are hesitant and lacking confidence. Processes are in limbo. Results remain potential. Things are unfinished. Failure to decide makes you and your team like a car in one of two conditions: You're either stuck in neutral (burning energy but not going anywhere), or you're going hard and fast down the wrong road (and need to turn around).

Decisiveness results in clear strategy, smart planning and (most importantly) action and execution. You and your team know what to do, how to do it and have a clear, shared picture in mind about the needed outcome.

Another component of decisiveness is sticking to your decision. If you've made an informed decision, then stand by it (unless you get different information). If you consistently waffle or change direction after making a decision, the outcome is very much like not deciding in the first place—including the effects on your team.

Make Informed Decisions

Decisions should be information-driven—assuming the information is available. When leaders fail to make informed decisions, it's usually because they are substituting other things for solid, actionable information. This could include things like emotions, pressures, habits, perceptions, expectations, history, self-interests, security or any number of other factors that shape our thinking.

Skilled leaders have the ability to discern and focus on the most critical and actionable information from the stream of details and stimuli coming at them. They also have an awareness of contingencies: An ability to consider additional opportunities, likely pitfalls and what to do if they arise.

> "When leaders fail to make informed decisions, it's usually because they are substituting other things for solid, actionable information."

Take All the Time You Need...

One of the rookie mistakes I often see is deciding too far in advance. Many decisions have a point in which the decision must be made. Prior to that point, these decisions may have no negative consequences. So why decide before it's necessary?

Taking time brings several big advantages. Perhaps the most basic advantage is it keeps you from being locked-in to an early strategy that may prove inadequate when conditions change. Taking time to decide also allows you to acquire additional information and provides you the opportunity for deeper thought on the subject.

Many times additional perspective and reflection will reveal strategies, opportunities or threats you didn't see before. Of course, you won't have this opportunity on every decision. But when the decision allows it, take all the time you need.

...But Don't Delay

There are several reasons decisions are delayed such as inadequate planning or waiting on others. These are situational and can affect any leader.

> "Many times additional perspective and reflection will reveal strategies, opportunities or threats you didn't see before."

But sometimes this trait is not situational; it's habitual. Some leaders have developed a habit of delayed decision-making. These leaders have simply become comfortable with waiting to decide. There's some tension between making timely decisions (not delaying) and informed decisions. One of the hard realities of decision-making is that sometimes the information you want simply isn't available. You must be prepared to deal with the unknowns, with incomplete, conflicting or imperfect information.

This tendency to delay often comes from the need (perceived or real) to remove every unknown. This is over-analysis, which has the effect of making no decision and is rightly called "paralysis by analysis." You, your team, your operation—everything—is paralyzed.

The outcomes of a lack of decision are more serious than they may appear, and they're not healthy. Consistent decision delays frustrate your team. They'll damage your credibility as a leader and undermine your team's willingness to trust you—the most foundational components of leadership.

Involve Others

This trait is largely about perspective: As one individual, you are limited in what you "see." Having additional perspective from others you trust helps you to see the full scope of the issue. Let me use a couple of visual metaphors to make my point.

First, it's easy to become narrow-focused. You end up "wearing blinders." Blinders are what trainers put on racehorses to keep them from being distracted by activity behind them or to their side. Being focused is a positive leadership behavior, but if your focus is so narrow and fixed that you don't see the breadth of everything that's in play, you'll miss obvious data that could impact the decision.

> "So how do you know the difference between being focused and wearing blinders?"

So how do you know the difference between being focused and wearing blinders?

Now that's a really good question.

The second metaphor is being myopic—short-sighted. This isn't as common as wearing blinders, but it can still happen. Leadership myopia comes when you become so fixed on short-term objectives that you lose sight of the long-term goal. You end up sighting on targets that won't ultimately lead to your desired destination (see Chapter 26 – Riding the Thin Line).

Wearing blinders and being short-sighted cause your decision-making to suffer. One blinds you to reality, and the other causes you to lose sight of your goal. Involving others brings additional perspective and more information. Seek out people who know what you don't or people who've been down this road before. Seek out trusted antagonists: People you trust, who you know will see things differently.

Admittedly for some decisions, more information can be counterproductive (and can push you into over-analysis). But for most decisions, it's essential. You'll have to filter out information that's irrelevant (or incorrect), but you'll very likely see things you'd otherwise miss.

There's one other point to make about involving others: Their involvement needs to be genuine. There's a difference between merely having others in the room as you share your decision and truly leveraging the input of others to make a decision. Sometimes, those leaders who are gifted, decisive decision-makers struggle with letting go of the opportunity to decide. They can even struggle with delegation because of their tendency to control the decision-making process.

> "[Your team needs] to learn how to decide. Don't give them the luxury of deciding for them."

If you find yourself heavily involved in the decisions of your team, or if you find your team has to come to you for approval on most of their decisions, this may be an indication that you need to give them more responsibility to make decisions. Meanwhile, you can concentrate more on coaching and evaluating their decision-making process. They need to learn how to decide. Don't give them the luxury of deciding for them.

Be Prepared to Stand Alone

There will be some decisions where no one will back you. Others will feel differently, see things you don't, flat out disagree with you or simply be too afraid to stand with you. They won't have access to the information you have, or they won't agree with the direction the decision will take. Whatever the cause, you'll be alone.

When these types of decisions occur, there are three things you'll find yourself leaning on to make good decisions: your gut, your head and your heart.

Your "Gut"

Your values and convictions will help you navigate through rough seas and tides that pull you off course. They're a foundation that keeps you on solid footing when everything around pressures you to go in a different direction. Because values represent what we believe to be true, we depend on them at a level that goes beyond mere information.

Of course, the more clarity you have of your values, the easier it is to lean on them. And if you don't know them, this will not be an area of strength for you.

Please let that thought sink in, and if necessary go back and (re)read Chapter 2 – Fit Happens.

Your "Head"

This is where your understanding—and particularly wisdom—comes into play. Wisdom is knowledge gained over time; it's knowledge put into practice. Wisdom comes from observing the outcome of similar situations in the past both in your personal experience and the experience of others. Wisdom and experience are wonderful teachers, and we only become their students when we allow them to influence our decisions.

> "…that's the nature of passion—it's personal and must be 'owned' at a personal level."

Your "Heart"

Passion is a drive, an energy, a determination, a motivation to pursue an outcome. Often, others will not share the same level of passion you do. They will give it lip service or will share only a degree of your passion.

But you should work to communicate it nonetheless. If you don't, you can come off looking like a Don Quixote or a Captain Ahab. If you do, be prepared for it to take some time and for people to need convincing. In the end, they may still not understand or relate to your passion.

Passion can result in a degree of isolation and, at times, even produce some disappointment. But that's the nature of passion— it's personal and must be "owned" at a personal level. You'll find that others sometimes simply won't own it. Passion is very much like vision: Others may not see it at first (or ever). And even when they do, they may not reach the same level of passion that you have.

> "Passion is very much like vision: Others may not see it at first (or ever)."

Practicing decision-making is one of the simplest, most practical ways to improve your leadership effectiveness—and it will have an almost immediate impact. It's tough to do well consistently, but it's usually easy to recognize your tendencies. Getting started at improving your decision-making can come pretty quickly.

As long as you decide to do it.

Put It in Motion

- **Be Decisive.** When the time is right for a decision, make it—and then stick to it unless something changes.

- **Make Informed Decisions.** Get as much of the right data as you can and consider any contingency situations.

- **Wait to Decide Until You Need To.** Deciding before it's necessary may prematurely limit your options downstream.

- **Make Timely Decisions.** Avoid paralysis by analysis, and don't let fear, anxiety or unknowns introduce a delay.

- **Deal With All the Tensions.** Often there is tension in each of the points above, and something's going to be compromised.

- **Involve Others Where Appropriate.** One person can't have all the insight. Besides, it's a great mentoring exercise.

15 – STARTS AND STOPS

"You can't blow an uncertain trumpet."
Theodore Hesburgh

One of my regular biking circuits includes First Avenue North and First Avenue South in St. Pete. They are separated by Central Avenue, which extends westward from downtown and, at one time, marked the center of life of the city when it was founded.

Today, "First Ave" (as the locals call it) forms a pair of one-way streets. Traffic on First Ave North flows west, and First Ave South runs east. The stoplights on each street are timed so you can drive the speed limit without stopping.

Back when I was riding The Beast (see Chapter 1), I found that First Ave North's stoplights were spaced where I could hit most of them when they were green. On the return leg on First Ave South, however, I caught almost every red light.

> "You lose more than momentum with stop-starts —you lose some leadership credibility."

When I shared this frustration with my wife (for whom the glass is always half full) before she took up riding herself, she commented, "Well, at least it gives you a chance to rest."

"Yeah, the rest is nice," I responded. "But it's the getting started again part that kills."

The restart forces you to get your heart rate up again. Breathing is difficult for the first minute or so. The legs stiffen up, and rhythm is lost along with time. And it takes an emotional toll to have to stop the momentum you just finished working so hard to build up.

The same is true for leadership. Losing momentum sucks the air out of your team's lungs. Restarting takes an emotional toll.

Extra energy has to be spent, which means productivity and results go down. Rhythm is lost, and it may take a while to find it again.

And don't forget: You lose more than momentum with stop-starts—you lose some leadership credibility. It's like a tax we levy on our team: If the restart is necessary and unavoidable, the tax is minimal; if the restart comes from poor strategy or sloppy execution, the tax can be steep. And no matter what the cause, the tax will be severe if restarts come at a high frequency. Your staff members are the ones pedaling the operations. So be wise about how many times you stop and start.

> "Remember, what looks like a great new idea to you might look like an unnecessary stop-start to your team."

Here are some questions that might help you avoid unnecessary restarts:

- Can you see patterns in your management that add to the loss of momentum?
- Do you know everything you can know? What other facts, options, opportunities, relationships, etc. are out there that you haven't taken the time to think of yet? Many times, disciplining yourself to ask, "What else?" or "What have we not thought of?" will uncover them.
- Do you know everything you need to know before you create and launch the plan? This is the other side of the "knowledge" coin: achieving an operational comfort level with the facts you have. You could spend more time in research and vetting, but will it add strategic value to the task? Unnecessary effort spent on confirmation and research is effort that could be spent on execution—and it feels like a stop-start to your team.
- What do your new strategies look like to those who are pedaling?
- If changes are necessary, what can you do to redirect without restarting? Can anything be done concurrently?
- If the change/stop-start is unavoidable, is there a way you can divert minimal resources so the main effort can continue (i.e., as a sort of R&D effort)?

- And if you've found some momentum—hitting all the lights when they're green—what can you do to sustain it?

Remember, what looks like a great new idea to you might look like an unnecessary stop-start to your team. Ultimately, you need to ask yourself the question: Is this new effort necessary to get us the results we need, or is it a distraction?

In a perfect world, there would be ample time and resources to do what needs to be done. But that's not the world we live and work in. That's what makes managing time and resources the artful competency it is.

> "Ultimately, you need to ask yourself the question: Is this new effort necessary to get us the results we need, or is it a distraction?"

It's ironic that sometimes stopping your bike ride is in fact *not* a good way to rest. Since restarts affect the body the way they do, an elongated stop is, in essence, like starting a whole new ride. Sometimes, the best way to get refreshed is simply to slow down. You can change your gearing so your cadence is less taxing. You can get caught up on some nutrition. You can change your body position by getting out of the saddle or taking your hands off the bars and sitting up straight (as if you were riding a unicycle). But by continuing the ride, you maintain progress and avoid the discomfort and difficulty of starting all over.

In the same way, stopping your team's work is often not the best way to rest. Your team is most productive and effective when it can sustain a natural rhythm. When rest is needed, let them rest while continuing to move forward wherever possible. Add some variety in tasks or take the opportunity for training, team building or vision casting to provide a needed break. But do whatever you can to avoid major redirects or stop-starts. You'll find they end up much further down the road.

Put It in Motion

- **Find a Rhythm and Stick to It.** Rhythm allows people to get into a flow of thought, action, communication, decision, analysis, etc., which all contribute to greater effectiveness.

- **Restarting is the Hard Part.** Driving hard organizationally is much easier when you're in rhythm.

- **Learn to Rest While Still Moving Forward.** You shouldn't constantly drive to exhaustion. Slowing down and adding intentional pace changes or task variety allow the team to breathe easier without having to stop altogether.

16 – PRACTICE DOESN'T MAKE PERFECT

"He who stops being better stops being good."
Oliver Cromwell

I'm an addict.

I'm, admittedly, hooked on improvement.

Maybe that's one of the reasons why riding a bike resonates with me: It invites development. For one, there's immediate and obvious performance feedback. With the right equipment, you can measure a variety of factors: speed, heart rate, time spent in a range or heart rate zones, pedaling cadence, power exerted and miles ridden. You can measure the averages from all these categories for a given ride and compare them to other rides.

You can also join riders who are stronger than you. The challenge of trying to keep up without being left behind—what's known in the cycling world as "getting dropped"—keeps you honest about your ability (both current and potential).

> *"...if you ride the same route (or same type of routes), the same way, at the same speed, with the same goal in mind ... you won't improve."*

But it's more than just the feedback. The experience of the ride always calls you to improve so the next experience can be even greater. It makes you want to get better; and the better you get the more you want to get better.

Addicting.

There are so many things that go into improving cycling performance and so many systems in the body (the heart, lungs, muscles, brain). Each part needs to be developed to its full potential. But how?

The first step is the most obvious: Getting better at cycling requires riding—a lot. The amount differs from one cyclist to the next, but no cyclist improves by sitting on the couch and thinking about riding. You have to get on the bike.

From here, things are more calculated. One of the things cycling teaches you is that it takes more than just getting out on the road. If you ride the same route (or same type of routes), the same way, at the same speed, with the same goal in mind … you won't improve. Even if you ride frequently, you'll be at the same level one year from now—plateaued.

One way to break out of plateauing is to vary your training regimen. Plan rides that are designed to improve a specific area of your ability, like average speed or distance. Other rides can be designed to target certain body systems, like your heart, legs, or level of endurance. The mix of training regimens strengthens each area in ways that merely working to perfect one area never could.

> "If you really want to get better, you can't keep practicing the things you're already good at."

This is not just a cycling phenomenon. The P90X® and Insanity® fitness workout systems currently on the market have caught on (and cashed in) to this idea. They call it "muscle confusion." Muscles tend to accommodate to the same exercise routine repeated over and over again, and development plateaus—even when muscles are pushed to fatigue each time. Continuing the same routine keeps the muscle in shape, but it doesn't add significant strength and endurance. They get strong, and then they stop getting stronger.

A varied approach constantly tasks the body to do things it's not accustomed to. It "thinks" it's in the beginning phases of development, and so it stays in an alert, "agile" mode. It's ready to grow and get better. The result is continued growth and increased strength and endurance.

The point? If you really want to get better, you can't keep practicing the things you're already good at.

Frankly, it's hard to get leaders to take the time for development.

First, it's additional work.

Second, the payoff often isn't immediate and frequently isn't direct.

Third, most serious areas of development require some increased vulnerability. Before you can get better, you first have to admit you *can* get better; you have to see the opportunity. This often means opening yourself to self-critique and feedback from others—not easy in the hyper-competitive culture we live in.

On top of that, development is fuzzy. It involves internalization and reflection. Many capable leaders are results-driven: They focus on producing results rather than taking some "inward journey" that appears to have limited concrete outcomes. Effort spent on development dilutes focus and energy away from getting results—which is how they are motivated and rewarded.

> "You only get better at leading by practicing it, developing as you go by incorporating practice into your regular leadership activity."

Perhaps the greatest reality is that development is never convenient. Rarely is there a season in which you find yourself with spare time to devote to "sharpening the saw."

The result is that in many organizations development comes as a crisis option. The usual scenario occurs when a leader's lack of development has affected results, and he/she now faces the pressure of a "develop-or-else" ultimatum—the most unproductive scenario for development.

Development is not something you do on the side. It's not something you do when the rest of your work is done—as if your work is ever "done."

You only get better at leading by practicing it, developing as you go by incorporating practice into your regular leadership activity. And the only practice that will improve your leadership is what Geoff Colvin, in his book *Talent is Overrated,* calls "deliberate practice." Deliberate practice is akin to muscle-confusing exercise: It's practicing with development in mind. Instead of practicing the things you're already good at, you purposefully design a regimen of activity designed to develop competencies that are not current strengths for you. It must be focused, intentional and include immediate feedback on your performance.

Your ultimate performance as a leader hinges on your development. If you don't develop, you won't ever perform at a higher level than you're at right now. The challenges always get bigger, margins always get tighter and resources scarcer as schedules compress and expectations increase. To choose to maintain your current level of leadership competency—to plateau—is to make a strategic decision for weakness and incompetency in your leadership future.

So, a question to ponder: Are you comfortable with that? If so, then you can move on to the next chapter ... or another book altogether. Or do nothing at all, because that's what's going to happen to your leadership effectiveness: nothing.

If that question makes you squirm, then truly the only option open to you is to choose to develop.

> "To choose to maintain your current level of leadership competency... is to make a strategic decision for weakness and incompetency in your leadership future."

Where to begin? That's a really, *really* good question. I applaud you for asking it. I'd start with Geoff Colvin's book, and I'd also recommend Marshall Goldsmith's *What Got You Here Won't Get You There*, which will help you identify your "blind spots" and misperceptions about your leadership behaviors.

If you want to get straight to the point, then you need a mirror to see yourself as you really are—the way others see you. This involves some kind of assessment, whether it's a full-blown 360° assessment or an informal review in which you ask trusted friends or colleagues to help you identify areas where you can improve your leadership performance.

Oh, and a word of caution: A good mirror will give you a true image of yourself as you really are. Be ready to see some things you may be uncomfortable talking about.

You should also be ready to see things you didn't expect to see—things you were blind to. Be prepared to hear comments that might surprise you. I encourage you not to react. Don't dismiss them or rationalize them away. It's easy to think someone's out to get you or is carrying a grudge. If you choose your evaluators wisely—people who have your best interests in mind and will provide honest, genuine feedback—then you'll get a solid, actionable image of your leadership competency.

And you'll know where you need to start.

From here on out, it's basic leadership activity—the same activity you undertake to accomplish anything else. It's having a vision. It's setting (deliberate) practice goals and objectives. It's establishing accountability and measuring progress. It's managing change.

> "...you need a mirror to see yourself as you really are—the way others see you."

Only this time it's about *changing you.*

If you want to get better, you must begin. Once you do, chances are you won't ever want to stop.

Put It in Motion

- **Don't Be Afraid of Development.** Everyone needs it—no matter how good of a leader they currently are.

- **You Only Get Better at Leading by Practicing It.** It takes more than just thinking about getting better. You have to actively engage in processes that will make you better.

- **Go Beyond the Things You're Already Good At.** You need to design in "deliberate practice" (thanks to Geoff Colvin) steps that will accelerate your development.

- **Incorporate Development into Your Regular Activity.** It's not something you do "on the side" or when you get the time.

- **Not Developing is a Strategy for Leadership Mediocrity.** If you don't develop, you won't ever perform at a higher level than you're at right now. And since the challenges always get bigger, you'll eventually lose ground.

17 – THE PELOTON

"The main ingredient of stardom is the rest of the team."
John Wooden

Before I started riding, from the outside looking in, I saw cycling as an intensely individual endeavor. There was one winner; he/she was first across the finish line. The winner wore the yellow jersey, made it all happen and took the glory.

Never have I been more wrong.

Teams—not individual riders—win races. Obviously, you have to be a great rider to wear yellow. But no great rider ever stood on the podium without a great team.

Part of this comes from the advantages of riding in a group. In cycling it's called the peloton, which is French for "platoon." The peloton is one of the most visible symbols of cycling. Riders form into a peloton for the same reason birds fly in formation: Riding together is easier. When competitors in a race choose to ride together, you know it's important.

> **"Riders form into a peloton for the same reason birds fly in formation: Riding together is easier."**

It's impossible for any one person to win a bike race. There's simply no way one person can have the capacity to accomplish all that's required to achieve victory.

Seeing the leadership application in a peloton is, hopefully, obvious. There are some key principles that come into play:

1. There's more to do than any one person can do
2. No one person has all the skills
3. Defining success in terms of the team and not the individual

4. Working together is more rewarding
5. Leading and managing others to success is your role

Let's take these one at a time.

There's More to Do

If the task is small, it's fine to DIY. But if the endeavor has any degree of complexity—and most big things in life do—then no one person can do it all.

Shared workload is the most obvious and basic advantage of teaming together versus going at it alone. In cycling, the best example of sharing workload is what's called a paceline. This is where a small group of riders line up tightly in single file (or sometimes double), and everyone maintains a constant pace.

> "The message is simple: Ride alone and you'll finish alone, beaten and tired and usually well off the pace."

The lead rider in a paceline will hold position for three to four seconds and then peel off and drift back as the paceline passes him. When this rider gets to back of the line, he takes up position in the rear of the paceline. The rider who took up the lead position then also peels off, and the process continues.

Pacelines are very effective since the work of riding in the front is shared and everyone gets a chance to rest when they're drafting in the group. The time spent in the lead varies with the speed of the group: The faster the pace the quicker the rotation.

Even as competitors, cyclists ride together in a paceline. Because of the unique nature of cycling, there's strength in numbers. It's extremely rare for any single rider to outperform a paceline, particularly on longer rides. Any rider who tries to go at it alone just can't keep up.

The message is simple: Ride alone and you'll finish alone, beaten and tired and usually well off the pace.

There's more to do in life and business than any one person can accomplish. Even if you can do *each* thing well (which most people can't), you can't do *everything* at once. The workload must be distributed and shared. Everyone must pitch in.

People need to be allowed to rotate out of the hardest jobs and be given a break every now and then. Everyone needs to keep the same pace.

Plus, the most critical point of this (from a leadership context) is so often missed: If you're spending time doing everything, you're not focusing on leading. And if you're not leading, who is?

No One Has All the Skills

Cycling teams are made up of people in a variety of roles. There's the team manager, the *directeurs sportifs* (French for "sporting director"), which direct the race strategies; the coaches and therapists, who manage training; the *soigneurs* ("one who provides care"), who handle daily basic care needs like food, clothing, etc.; and the mechanics, who repair the bikes and keep them in top order.

The riders themselves have unique skills and abilities that allow them to excel at different race specialties (like sprinting or climbing), which I'll elaborate on in Chapter 18 – Know Who You Are (and Who You're Not). Perhaps the most intriguing—and vital—role on a cycling team is the

> "It takes a diversity of talent, attitudes, motivations and capacities. And getting them all to work together requires you to have a genuine appreciation for each role..."

domestique (French for "servant"). To put it simply, domestiques do whatever needs to be done to help the team succeed. They ride in "lead outs," which means when their team attacks or breaks away from the pack, they ride in front allowing the team's lead rider to draft behind them until the end of the race. They push ahead to catch other breakaways. They fall back to offer assistance (and sometimes even their bikes) to the rider who's leading the race. They bring refreshments to their teammates.

Each of these roles is absolutely essential for a team to win. If any of them is not filled and performed capably, no team will win. But here's the key: No one person can perform in all of these roles. It takes a diversity of talent, attitudes, motivations and capacities. And getting them all to work together requires you to have a genuine appreciation for each role and respect for each person in those roles.

> "...you must describe and define success in terms of the team and not anyone's personal victory—especially your own."

Leadership, at some point, requires that you think "team" and manage and value individuals for both the role they fill as well as how these individuals integrate to function effectively.

Not identifying the roles needed as well as putting people in the wrong roles will almost guarantee a lack of success. This is Jim Collins' famous admonition, "Get the right people on the bus, the wrong people off the bus, and the right people in the right seats."

Defining Success in Terms of the Team

One of the traditions in major cycling races around the world is for the race winner to split the first place earnings equally with the team. Though one person wears yellow, it's the team that produces the victory.

This is a wonderful example of the leadership perspective. Once it's clear that A) there's more to do than any one person can accomplish, and B) no one person has the skills to accomplish everything there is to accomplish, is there any other way to view success other than in the context of a team? If not, then minimize (if not discard) the visions of individual success and replace them with visions of a winning team.

As the leader, you should take every possible opportunity to reinforce this perspective. First, in your own mind and then on an ongoing basis with the team you lead, you must describe and define success in terms of the team and not anyone's personal victory—especially your own.

There are activities that are individual in nature and must be faced individually. And individuals (you included) will experience fulfillment and achievement. I don't mean to diminish these in any way. But the truly elusive and greatest challenges to overcome in life require a team. And so success, in its grandest expression, is shared.

Riding Together is More Rewarding

Aside from the strategic part of team cycling, there's a basic, inescapable observation: The miles always pass quicker when riding with others.

Cycling can be a very communal activity. There's so much sharing, interaction, support and camaraderie in riding. I still enjoying riding alone, but I much prefer to ride with others.

> "We need to belong—to live and work with our people. We need a tribe. If we don't have one, we wither."

Americans, in particular, value individuality. Or, probably more accurately, we idolize it. Take a look at almost any action movie. More often than not, the hero or heroine is a go-at-it-alone, hide-your-vulnerability, fiercely-independent personality. We've created an image of heroism that is intensely individual—and isolating.

But what works in the movies doesn't work in real life. Isolation is destructive; it's a cancer.

It's easy at first. You don't have to deal with personalities or other people's issues. You don't have to work to convince others. You don't have to step easy so as not to offend. You don't have to apologize or watch the way you say things. You don't have to be vulnerable.

Easier.

But then isolation can begin to eat away at you. You begin to question, to doubt. You become resentful. You become inwardly focused. You lose hope. You end up dissatisfied and bitter with nothing to point to as the cause.

Humans are communal beings. We need to belong—to live and work with our people. We need a tribe. If we don't have one, we wither. Why do you think solitary confinement is one of the worst punishments criminals or prisoners can face?

Eventually, isolation will destroy you.

If you're an established, experienced leader, then find a new leader to mentor. Give them some of your time and wisdom. Help them navigate through the early part of their journey, where everything seems to come so fast and from so many directions.

If you're a new leader and you don't have a mentor, find one. Don't be afraid or ashamed to ask for help. It's not a sign of weakness; it's a sign of courage and wisdom.

> "...ultimately, the best remedies for isolation are the relationships on your team."

No matter where you are on your leadership continuum, you'll also benefit from working with a leadership coach. It's beneficial to have someone outside your circle with whom you can discuss your situation to get perspective and encouragement.

But, ultimately, the best remedies for isolation are the relationships on your team. My experience tells me that having a genuine team experience is rare. A minority of teams have relationships that are close-knit, strong and mutually respectful, with people who genuinely appreciate and complement each other and enjoy working together—whether or not they "like" each other. While it may be more rare, once you've experienced it, you won't settle for anything less. Never stop seeking to create this kind of team environment.

Because it's always more rewarding to ride together.

It's Your Role

Perhaps the best way to sum up the importance of the peloton is to remember that leading and managing others to success is what a leader is supposed to do. Doug Rauch, former President of Trader Joe's, poignantly recalls a time where this became crystalized in his mind:

> Bringing Trader Joe's from the West Coast to the East meant we had to hire an entirely new staff. We had to teach everyone the Trader Joe's buying philosophy, the organizational culture, the details that made us successful. In my mind, no one could do that better than I could, because no one else had the knowledge I did. I happily micromanaged the expansion.

> A year or so in, they'd gotten my message just fine. The culture was instilled, the philosophy bought into. Only I didn't see it. In my zeal to control everything, I failed to notice that it was time to take off the training wheels and let the new staff members grow into their roles. I kept micromanaging. The effect was stifling, especially on our buyers, the heart of our organization…

> Luckily for me, one intrepid senior buyer helped put a stop to all this. She approached me and said, "You're driving us crazy. You've got to back off. We'll make mistakes, but you've got to let us go."

> "…winning through others is much more rewarding and satisfying than trying to win alone."

> …As I worked on letting go, I came to see micromanaging as a failure to let others shine or grow. So instead of fixing problems, I focused on nurturing problem solvers. I turned "Try this" into "What do you think we should try?" I replaced the satisfaction of doing something myself, the way I wanted it done, with the joy of watching others do something their way and succeed.[3]

You are in the position to inspire, equip and release your peloton to be successful. Even if you wanted to do it all, you can't. You don't have all the skills, and even if you did, you can't leverage them to success the way a team can.

---

[3] Rauch, Doug. "Failure Chronicles." *Harvard Business Review*, Apr. 2011. Web.

Besides, winning through others is much more rewarding and satisfying than trying to win alone.

Put It in Motion

- **There's More to Do Than Any One Person Can Do.** No one person can accomplish it all. Even if you can do *each* thing (which most people can't), you can't do *everything* at once.

- **If the Leader is Overinvolved in the Work, Who's Leading?** (*No elaboration required*)

- **No One Person Has All The Skills.** In efforts of moderate size or complexity, it's extremely rare to find one person who excels at everything. A diverse collection of experience, skills, personalities and perspectives is required.

- **Define Success in Terms of the Team.** When you imagine success, think "team" and not "individual"—yourself included. Doing this bakes in good team management on your part.

- **Working Together is More Rewarding.** It's not necessarily easier, but it's more rewarding and fulfilling. Isolation is a quiet leadership cancer that raises levels of stress and anxiety and reinforces ineffective relational patterns in people.

- **It's Your Role.** Seems like such a basic point, doesn't it? Yet this is an area that many leaders fall down on. That's what makes effective leadership so special.

---

18 – KNOW WHO YOU ARE
(AND WHO YOU'RE NOT)

"Reflection is looking in so you can look out with a broader, bigger, and more accurate perspective."
Mick Ukleja and Robert Lorber

Riders come in all different types. There are some riders who are tailor-made sprinters. British cyclist Mark Cavendish is a great example of a professional sprinter. Known as the Manx Missile (he comes from the Isle of Mann in the U.K.), he's the first rider in the history of the Tour de France to win the final stage at Paris' Champs-Élysées four times in a row. He's aggressive (accused at times of being too aggressive). He has an amazing ability to position himself at the end of a race in just the right spot at just the right time. He has a gift of sensing when to pour it on—not too early and not too late.

Nairo Quintana is a climber. He was a new rider on the 2013 Tour de France. He won stage 20, which finished at the ski station above the town of Annecy Semnoz. The stage covered 125 kilometers (78 miles) and gained 912 meters (about 3,000 feet) in altitude—an average grade of 8.5%. What was so striking during this ride was his appearance. He was comfortable and in control. There was no appearance of struggle, while all the other riders seemed to be working hard, wrestling with the mountain and hanging on. He, very obviously, looked like he was just out for a ride.

> "...you have to know yourself and be able to use your natural style and gifts to your best advantage."

In cycling, there are different types of riders. There are sprinters, time-trialists and climbers. There are also great all-around riders, who are not exceptional at any one specialty but who are pretty good at everything.

When you're competing against the elite riders of the world, you have to know yourself and be able to use your natural style and gifts to your best advantage.

> "The more you're aware of who you are, the better equipped you will be to maximize your influence..."

The same holds true for leadership. Leaders come in all different shapes and types. Some are entrepreneurial, and they are uniquely wired to start things no one else has thought of. Other leaders are organizers, who can take a team in chaos and establish systems, remove inefficiencies and make it a well-oiled machine. Still others are motivators, whose greatest asset is their ability to inspire and empower, help people to embrace and adopt a vision and create a contagious, "can't lose" moxie in the organization.

Know Thyself

Your influence is expressed in terms of your natural style and giftedness. The more you're aware of who you are, the better equipped you will be to maximize your influence with your team and leverage your gifts.

Your natural style includes your "hard-wiring": Your natural personality and temperament that, in all likelihood, will never change. Are you energized by people or by things and tasks? Are you philosophical or practical? Do you see things through the lens of facts and data or through ideas and feelings? Are you outgoing and expressive or quiet, internal and reflective? Are you competitive, and focused on achievement and getting it done? Or are you more focused on the process by which you achieve results? Do you prefer to be in front of people, getting them excited and trying to build camaraderie? Or are you driven by high standards and details? Are you a mix? There are numerous, inexpensive assessment tools on the market to help give you a sense of your hard-wiring like the Myers-Briggs Type Indicator or the DiSC Temperament Style assessment.

Your leadership has been shaped by your experience—what you've seen and done before. Obviously, you can't prepare for everything in advance. But equally obvious is that you want to be as prepared as possible to handle what you might encounter. That's why it's important for new leaders to work through a variety of situations—some that will stretch them beyond their comfort zone—so they will have a breadth of experience to draw from when needed.

Another part of knowing who you are is to know who you are not. You can't be great at everything; all leaders have some blind spots: areas of their behavior they don't see that decrease their effectiveness. Having blind spots is nothing to be ashamed of because it's a part of being human—but you need to know you have them so you can be aware and change those behaviors.

Because you can't be great at everything, you must develop the discipline of surrounding yourself with people who are what you are not (see Chapter 17 – The Peloton and Chapter 23 – You've Got More Resources Than You Think). You want people you can trust, who are strong in areas you are not and who see things a little bit differently. Work with them enough to trust their instincts so they become an extension of your leadership. Organizations suffer when they become too homogenous and there's not enough diversity.

> "You can't be great at everything; all leaders have some blind spots: areas of their behavior they don't see that decrease their effectiveness."

Manage AND Lead

The terms "management" and "leadership" have often been misunderstood and so misapplied. Peter Drucker perhaps most clearly lays out the contrast between the two: "Management is doing things right. Leadership is doing the right things."

Management results in *standardization*. Leadership, in contrast, results in *transformation*. Look at the chart below to see how the two roles compare (thanks to Dave Logan for highlighting the contrast).

Management *Doing Things Right*	Leadership *Doing the Right Things*
Standardization	Transformation
Processes	Purpose
Improvement	Innovation
Efficiency	Effectiveness
Measurement	Achievement
How? Who? When?	What? Why?
Systems/Policies	Goal Achievement
From "Chaos" to "Order"	From "Stuck" to "Agile"
Eliminate the Unknowns	Explore the Unknowns
Detailed Analysis	Big Picture Analysis
Micro Adjustments	Macro Adjustments
Tactical	Strategic

Some situations require a management-centric approach. For example, when teams are lacking established processes, can't measure their activity, can't repeat their successes, can't sustain their results and are out of sync and flailing … these are all signs that they need more and better management.

Other situations require a leadership-centric approach. Some organizations desperately need transformation: They are without purpose, are stuck doing things "the way they've always been done," are devoid of vision or noble cause, with an extinct paradigm for why they exist and what they do. There are teams driven by compliance to rules or traditions that have long since lost their relevance. These are all signs that they need more and better leadership.

If you try to fix a management problem with leadership solutions, you'll fail—miserably. And if you try to fix a leadership problem with management solutions, the results will be equally disastrous. Each situation requires the right solution.

Here's the main point: Naturally speaking, you have a predominant approach of being either a manager OR a leader.

Your natural make-up will push you toward defaulting to one side or the other—rare is the person who is naturally strong at both.

Think of it as becoming ambidextrous. Many years ago I broke my right arm—my dominant writing hand. I learned pretty quickly to write with my left hand. It wasn't pretty at first (and never was as clear as my right), but it was adequate for the task.

Situations will likely require the application of both leadership AND management so it's a matter of what you emphasize rather than doing one or the other. You want to develop the ability to be competent at both disciplines in a complementary way. It's possible, but you have to be intentional about it. It won't come naturally because it's not your "dominant hand." But it will make a big difference in your ability to be effective at influencing your team.

> "Knowing yourself allows you to relax—to be 'comfortable in your own skin.' Instead of trying to force yourself into a role that doesn't fit, the role comes to you."

Stay Within Yourself

You see it in sports all the time: when athletes attempt to perform in areas that don't play to their strengths. Football quarterbacks try to scramble, when they should stay in the pocket. Baseball pitchers try to throw harder, when their natural skill is to maintain their pitch command.

When you *know* yourself, you're able to *be* yourself. When you try to be someone we're not, it comes off as fake—inauthentic. It looks to others like you're trying too hard or perhaps that things are forced or unnatural. It's like wearing clothes that don't fit, pants that are too long and a shirt with sleeves too short: It looks goofy.

Everyone sees it even though they may not be able to explain it. It's part of our human ability to pick up on behavioral signs intuitively, subconsciously. When you're not comfortable with yourself, other people become uncomfortable with you. And when this happens, their natural response is to pull away and withhold their trust.

And losing trust is death to a leader.

Knowing yourself allows you to relax—to be "comfortable in your own skin." Instead of trying to force yourself into a role that doesn't fit, the role comes to you.

In that sense, there's no perfect approach to leadership—except the one that matches who you are.

Put It in Motion

- **Know Your Natural "Wiring."** Your personality, interests, motivators, passions and experience all combine to make you a unique leader. The more you know yourself, the better you'll be able to leverage your natural gifts to your best advantage.

- **Surround Yourself With Some People Not Like You.** They will see things you don't and create ideas you can't.

- **Manage And Lead.** It's about the "and" instead of the "or." The best leaders do both even if they more naturally do one or the other. You must do both because organizations need both. Incidentally, …

- **Don't Buy Into a Low View of Management.** Some people minimize being a "manager" as they promote the higher role of "leading." Frankly, I think that's foolish.

- **Stay Within Yourself.** You can adapt your approach without trying to be someone you're not. When you try to be someone you're not, it looks fake and is almost always less effective.

19 – PRESUME NOTHING

"Success is a lousy teacher.
It seduces smart people into thinking they can't lose."
Bill Gates

I was on a one-hour ride, which I approached as a time trial of sorts. I rode out as hard and as fast as possible for 30 minutes then turned around and tried to beat my time on my return leg. On this day, my outbound leg was unusually strong—four mph faster than my previous best.

I felt strong the entire time. When I dialed in for an extra push, my legs answered the call. I dug deep, and instead of the expected lactic acid burn, I discovered strength and resiliency. Breathing came steady and unlabored, and landmarks flew by in a blur.

So that's what this feels like!

I reached the 30-minute mark, traveling further and feeling better than any previous one-hour ride. I chalked it up to consistent training and good nutrition finally paying off. All was right in the world until I turned around and began my inbound leg—into a stiff headwind.

> "It's dangerous for leaders to be presumptuous about success."

Needless to say, my return leg time was less than remarkable. But beyond the results, my psyche was the greatest casualty. I found myself disengaging. I was self-critical. I felt naïve and defeated. It was a terrible experience after the high of the outbound leg. It was a difficult lesson to learn.

It's dangerous for leaders to be presumptuous about success. It could produce several disastrous results such as...

The Roller Coaster Effect

Presuming success often means getting blindsided. Since you aren't aware that you're working with a tailwind, you're ill-prepared to manage things when the wind direction changes and success becomes harder to achieve.

You most likely haven't prepared your team, and they aren't prepared for loss of momentum. It can quickly become a source of discouragement, distraction, disengagement and conflict. This all means additional work for you, of course. But the biggest impact is to your team and their output. It can take a long time for them to get back in sync and return to their previous level of performance.

> "Sometimes serendipity smiles on us, and things just work. But most of the time, things happen for a reason."

The Missed Opportunity

If you're unaware of what brought you success, you've most likely missed something that could be leveraged. Maybe it was something in the corporate environment or the market conditions. Perhaps there are skill sets on your team you didn't realize were there.

It could have been any number of things. But the point is this: It was something—so find out what it was. Sometimes serendipity smiles on us, and things just work. But most of the time, things happen for a reason. Quality leaders relentlessly find these things and then look for ways to capitalize on them.

The Leadership Credibility Hit

When your team encounters a sudden, unexpected headwind, you run the risk of appearing unrealistic and out of touch as a leader. At a minimum, their confidence in you is undermined. In more severe instances their ability to trust you may be affected—the worst possible outcome. Lack of trust in a leader is cancerous and overcoming it requires an immense amount of intentional effort and a consistent leadership performance on your part.

> "Lack of trust in a leader is cancerous and overcoming it requires an immense amount of intentional effort and a consistent leadership performance..."

There's another discipline that good leaders incorporate into success: performing a lessons-learned process. We typically think of performing lessons-learned sessions as after-action reviews when things go bad. But when we achieve success we often skip the process. We presume that success was a result of effective planning and hard work, when there may have been other unforeseen factors involved.

To be clear—this chapter is about *not presuming* upon success. That isn't the same thing as *celebrating* success. It's appropriate—and vital—that you stop to recognize, reflect and reward success and achievement. Doing so creates milestones and markers on the team's journey that serve as encouraging reminders, when things go into the weeds and your team gets overwhelmed.

This idea of presuming upon success goes hand-in-hand with Chapter 20 – Don't Get Caught Leaning. Sometimes you can take off down a path with a strategy built on "valid" assumptions that presumably brought you success the last time. But time and circumstance have a vetting process all their own; and what looked like boldness on the outbound leg, is proven to be something different when you lose your tailwind.

> "...what looked like boldness on the outbound leg, is proven to be something else when you lose your tailwind."

Your current strategy might be based on valid assumptions.

Then again …

Put It in Motion

- **Past Success Doesn't Guarantee Future Success.** Treat each situation you encounter as if it were a new opportunity—because it will be.

- **Your Team Bears the Brunt of Surprises.** Getting caught by surprise challenges can be demoralizing and distracting for your team.

- **If You Don't Know Why You Succeeded, You Can't Leverage It in the Future.** It sets the stage for being more presumptive in the future.

- **Avoid the Credibility Hit.** Being unprepared for surprise environmental changes ultimately reflects—perhaps even unfairly—on your credibility.

- **Do a Lessons Learned.** Make debriefing a regular business process, whether you succeed or fail.

---

20 – DON'T GET CAUGHT LEANING

"Nothing stops an organization faster than people who believe that the way you worked yesterday is the best way to work tomorrow."
Jon Madonna

So far, I've only crashed on my bike once.

I was riding on a stretch of four lane road in St. Pete with no center turn or bike lane. I was in the extreme right hand side, where the asphalt pavement meets the concrete gutter.

I try to avoid four-lane streets like this—for obvious reasons. But in this case, it was the best road to the bike trail, and I only had to ride it for one-half mile.

In this space of road, you deal with competing pressures. You want to give cars space to get around you, but you also want to stay out of the gutter that's frequently home to rocks, sticks, nails and untold types of debris that detract from the riding experience. This makes for a narrow riding zone.

"...when you lean on a bike, you tend to go in that direction—because leaning almost always trumps steering."

It was late afternoon so there was enough traffic on the road to make me uncomfortable. I had just left a stoplight and had gone about two blocks, getting up to cruising speed. A car passed me in my lane—which always makes me cringe.

That's probably what caused me to lean slightly toward the curb, which I attempted to correct by steering slightly back to the left. But when you lean on a bike, you tend to go in that direction—because leaning almost always trumps steering. So even though I was steering slightly to the left to avoid the gutter, my momentum continued to pull me toward the right.

My front tire then caught the lip of the pavement-concrete seam, jerking my wheel slightly to the left. This, combined with my center of mass moving progressively to the right, meant that I was now ballistic and a prisoner to gravity. That's when time stood suddenly, drastically still.

It's amazing how many things can go through your mind at times like this. It wasn't quite my entire life, but I do remember feeling like an idiot and wondering who was watching. I could already hear the concern of passersby, "Are you okay? Should we call 911?" I remember wondering what I was going to say to my wife, Cheryl, whose fear of riding on streets I had to appease (more than once)—"Don't worry; nothing's going to happen." I remember wondering what kind of bike repair costs I would be facing. I think I considered the potential market for selling cycling helmets with faceguards and shorts with hip pads.

> "We have tendencies, assumptions, preferences … things that add a certain inertia to our approach to leadership and decision-making."

After this instantaneous half-hour inward reflection, I hit the ground and was thrown onto the sidewalk. Fortunately, I landed on a pile of oak leaves that semi-cushioned my embrace with the concrete. I came away with a nice case of road rash on my elbow, knee and hip—along with a renewed sense of appreciation for bike helmets. The only damage to my bike was a slight bend in the brake handle and a skid mark on the saddle.

I stood up, looked around and was amazed (actually relieved) that no one, apparently, saw me. No cars were behind me, and no one was out in their yards. I picked my pride up off the ground, tucked in my embarrassment, got back on the bike and pedaled away.

And I also made a promise to myself: Never again would I get caught leaning in the wrong direction.

Leaders have a habit of leaning. It's natural and not necessarily a bad thing. We have tendencies, assumptions, preferences … things that add a certain inertia to our approach to leadership and decision-making.

In leadership as in cycling, leaning usually trumps steering. By that I mean our momentum often determines the direction and even overrides "steering" our team (steering meaning active leadership behaviors like giving direction, correcting, delegating, challenging, etc.).

In leadership, leaning is equivalent to operative assumptions: assumptions you've built your operational approach and strategies around. They're often so basic and deeply entrenched in your psyche and leadership approach that you probably aren't conscious of them.

In a business context, this might include assumptions like:
- The demand for our product or service will remain constant
- The direction of the board will be consistent
- The relationship with our suppliers will remain strong
- My aggressive approach to leading delivers results
- Satisfied customers will renew their contract with us
- My employees will remain engaged and productive
- People will continue to perform as they are directed
- What worked at my previous company will work in my new company
- Overthinking is unnecessary

In a personal context, it could be assumptions like:
- My relationship with my spouse will not change
- My children's interests and attitudes will be the same as mine
- Real estate is a good investment
- I'm good at telling others what to do
- There's nothing I haven't seen
- I'm not going to have any health challenges
- Doing [insert behavior here] has never hurt me before
- What could go wrong?

> "[Assumptions are] often so basic and deeply entrenched in your psyche and leadership approach that you probably aren't conscious of them."

These seem pretty basic, right? No brainers?

Yet, how many times do you see plans failing because people or organizations assumed something was true when it was not?

I'll say it again: Assumptions are often so basic and deeply entrenched you probably aren't conscious of them. They likely brought success in the past. The trap comes in assuming the environment that contributed to your previous success will remain constant.

And in fact, it might. Then again, you might find yourself leaning in the direction of your assumptions, when the environment suddenly changes or obstacles appear that you're unprepared to deal with. At this point, the wrong steering adjustment can be disastrous.

> "The trap comes in assuming the environment that contributed to your previous success will remain constant."

Had I been more aware, I would have briefly steered my bike in the direction I was leaning, gone safely across the gutter seam, corrected my lean and been able to steer back onto the asphalt without incident. But I took the easy way out (from an effort perspective) and moved the handlebar without correcting my lean.

It comes down to two principles:

1. **You must lean *AND* steer in the same direction.** If you don't, your momentum carries you one way and your steering the other—never a good combination. Or to say it positively, leaning *AND* steering in the same direction accelerates the direction change.

2. **Watch which way your leadership is leaning.** Don't let your momentum carry you in a direction that doesn't match up with the environment. The direction you're leaning is probably where you'll end up—because leaning almost always trumps steering.

I'm not suggesting that assumptions are a bad thing. I'm only saying to be aware of them. Challenge and interrogate them to confirm they're still valid. Otherwise, you'll be leaning the wrong way when a challenge—or an opportunity—presents itself.

Make a promise to yourself today: Don't get caught leaning in the wrong direction.

Put It in Motion

- **Leaning Almost Always Trumps Steering.** Your "leaning" (operative assumptions) has more inertia than your "steering" (leadership behaviors like planning, directing, communicating, etc.) because your strategy is usually based on your assumptions (whether you realize it or not).

- **You Probably Aren't Even Aware of Your Operative Assumptions.** They're usually deeply entrenched and have probably brought you success in the past.

- **Environments Change and So Must Your Assumptions.** Assumptions are not bad unless they're outdated and have become invalid.

- **You Want to Lean and Steer in the Same Direction.** When your assumptions and your leadership behaviors align, momentum and productivity accelerates.

- **The Direction You're Leaning is Probably the Direction You Will Go.** Being aware of your operative assumptions allows you to recognize if they're appropriate for the current environment.

21 – FACING A HEADWIND

"Nothing will ever be attempted if
all possible objections must first be overcome."
Samuel Johnson

The human body, when positioned on a bike, is not very aerodynamic. In fact, it acts like a parachute. When you're just cruising along at slow speeds, this doesn't matter. As you pick up your pace and ride faster, you start to become more aware of it. There's one situation, however, in which the aerodynamic inefficiency of the human body becomes painfully evident: when you ride into a headwind.

A headwind is a cruel slap in the face—a ball and chain. It's an emotional shot to the gut. It's the antagonist in the plot; like Mayhem for a rider, it relishes syphoning your energy and demoralizing you.

Wind tunnel tests show that if you're riding into a headwind that's identical to your current speed (e.g. you're maintaining 15 mph into a 15 mph headwind), it's not just twice as hard—it's *four times* as hard! You have to apply four times the power you would on a calm day. And the faster you try to go, the greater the challenge becomes.

> "You have to apply four times the power you would on a calm day."

Of course, there are numerous things you can do to fight a headwind. You can counter the resistance by changing the way your body hits the wind. You can move your hands down to the drops on your handlebar. Time trial or triathlon bikes are fit with handlebars that allow the rider to lean forward onto their elbows and put their hands together out in front. You can ride with your knees in, grazing the top tube of the frame and limiting the exposure of your inner thighs to the wind.

The best thing to do, of course, is to train for it. Expect it and don't be surprised by it. Get accustomed to—even comfortable with—riding into the wind. Allow it to challenge your body and mind. The more you train, the more disciplined and less vulnerable you'll be to the emotional impact of facing a headwind.

Like it or not a headwind is an inescapable part of riding. If you're going to sit in the saddle, sooner or later you're going to face a headwind. To ignore it, to hope it doesn't happen or to wish upon a star that you get a tailwind for life is naïve.

> "The more you train, the more disciplined and the less vulnerable you'll be to the emotional impact of facing a headwind."

Got a headwind? Bring it on.

Leadership has its own headwind: Resistance from the people you're leading.

This may come as a shock to you, but a time will come when the people you're leading will resist you. The level of resistance will fluctuate. The direction of resistance will vary. Even people who support you and value your leadership most will, at times, resist.

It can be demoralizing to leaders. When you least expect it—and often can least afford it—resistance hits you right in the face. Your progress slows. You have to expend additional energies you haven't budgeted for to keep your progress and pace on target. It beats you and drains you. You get out of sync. At a time when you most need your team to work efficiently and at the top of their game, they hesitate or stumble. Suddenly, even the stars on your team act like they've taken a stupid pill. Before long, they balk; they begin pushing back. They whine, and you become be the source of their pain.

Unfortunately, resistance can often have its biggest impact at the times you need it least: when you're driving hard and pushing to meet a deadline or that critical time when you're working hard to introduce strategic changes that will take your team or organization to the next level.

As the stakes go up and your patience goes down, the tendency is to get creative to try to deal with resistance. You might take a risk on behaviors that are out of the norm for you. Perhaps you get more intense or even desperate. You can try to light a fire under people, but if not done effectively, you can end up setting the situation on fire and burning someone.

Of course, there are things you can do. You can counter the resistance by increasing communication. Seasoned leaders know how to read their people and catch the early warning signs of resistance before it festers. You can build additional communication opportunities—which, in the moment, is probably the thing you least feel like doing. But more communication (rather than less) almost always helps. Budget time with your people and increase your availability. This is difficult to do if you haven't planned for it ahead of time—as it is, you're already expending additional energies to "go faster."

The best thing to do, of course, is to train for it. Expect it and don't be surprised by it. Get accustomed to—even comfortable with—riding into resistance. Allow it to challenge you. The more you train, the more disciplined you become and the less vulnerable you are to the emotional impact of facing resistance.

> "The best thing to do, of course, is to train for it. Expect it and don't be surprised by it."

Like it or not, resistance is an inescapable part of leading. If you're going to sit in the leadership saddle, sooner or later you're going to face resistance. To ignore it, to hope it doesn't happen or to wish upon a star that you get constant acceptance from those you lead is naïve.

There are three closing thoughts about resistance that are important to keep in mind. The first is that dealing with resistance doesn't mean just tolerating it all the time. You'll probably have to push back (dare I say "lead") at some point on those resisting you. That usually means things like:

- Giving them information they didn't have
- Providing additional context
- Encouraging them for the work they've done previously
- Coaching and asking a lot of open-ended questions
- Exploring to see if there's a *real* reason behind their resistance—you may have to dig for the truth rather than take their reasoning at face value

- Confronting inappropriate attitudes or helping them see their own shortcomings (don't go here unless it's called for and avoid going here first)

Dealing with resistance doesn't mean being passive; it's engaging and requires targeted, responsive (not reactive) behavior on your part.

The second thought is that you should always be prepared to adjust your position based on the feedback you're getting. Even if you're 99% right, making that small 1% adjustment on your part can make a big difference to diffusing the resistance. Plus remember—you might learn something; this is a chance for you to get better.

"...resistance from your team doesn't make them bad people. It makes them normal."

The final thought is that resistance from your team doesn't make them bad people. It makes them normal. Even the best of leaders with the most dedicated, all-in followers will encounter resistance—particularly when there's a high degree of change involved. Think about it, do you really want a team of robotic yes-folk, who never bring you alternatives, take a stand or view things from a different perspective than you? Do you want a team that can be unquestioningly driven until they collapse from fatigue?

The people you lead are just that: people. They'll never agree with you 100%. At times, will they resist because you've changed their routine? Yes. But resistance is a part of human nature. All leaders need to be able to lead through resistance.

If leading was easy, anyone could do it.

To ignore resistance, to hope it doesn't happen or to wish upon a star that you get constant acceptance from those you lead is naïve; it's delusional.

Got resistance? Bring it on.

Put It in Motion

- **Expect Resistance.** Prepare for it. Even your strongest performers and those who are most on board with your vision will resist you from time to time.

- **Resist the Temptation to Get Overly Creative.** You can't ignore it, but you shouldn't let it push you into behaviors that appear desperate or out of the norm for you.

- **Look for the Early Warning Signs.** Confusion, pushback, lack of engagement, side glances, tones of voice, excuses, lack of follow-through, poor attention to details, etc.—these may be signs that resistance is coming.

- **Keep Up Your Communication.** Make yourself available—especially for informal communication opportunities—and budget extra time with your team.

- **Even the Best of Team Members Resist.** Resisting is a part of human nature. Leading through resistance is something every leader needs to be able to do.

22 – THE WALL IS REAL (AND HITTING IT HURTS)

"Fatigue makes cowards of us all."
Vince Lombardi

It's a predator, and it's out there—waiting. It ambushes the inexperienced first; they're easy targets. Then it goes for the unprepared and distracted ones. And it gets everyone if they aren't ready.

You're going along fine, feeling strong. Then without warning it hits. Or, more accurately, you hit it—the wall.

> "It's the equivalent of a car running out of gas: The engine sputters and then just stops. Except the human body isn't quite that simple."

Cyclists and endurance athletes call it bonking[4]. It's a condition in which the body has depleted all its available energy. It's the equivalent of a car running out of gas: The engine sputters and then just stops. Except the human body isn't quite that simple.

I experienced bonking when (no surprise here) I began to go on longer rides. I'd led a fairly active lifestyle, playing a variety of sports over the years. But to my knowledge, I'd never bonked until I got into cycling. At first, I thought I was out of shape and that I needed to "toughen up." But as I began to study it, I realized there's more going on physically than I ever realized.

The liver stores glycogen, which the body then converts to glucose—the energy source that muscle cells need to function.

---

[4] Be careful using this term if you're in other cultures, such as in England where "bonk" means having sexual intercourse.

Glucose is also stored in fat cells, but (unfortunately, for those of us who would like to lose some extra pounds) the conversion doesn't happen quickly or easily.

When the available glucose from the liver is gone, the body gets desperate and starts robbing other sources for nourishment. When it can't find glucose, it tries to burn substitute sources like proteins. It tries, but nothing else works like glucose.

Bonk.

When it happens, anything requiring effort is a problem. Weakness overcomes you, and it feels like you're operating on an emergency generator in a power outage. A veil drops over your senses; things get cloudy, and simple thoughts get difficult. Many people feel nauseated; others get disoriented. It's not something you can gut out. Although you need to dismount and rest, resting alone doesn't cure it. Drinking water doesn't help. Nutrition is the only cure.

> "More often than not, it's the uninitiated and undisciplined who bonk."

You need food, specifically simple carbohydrates. When you get them, the body does its job and in about 20 minutes you're ready to go again.

The curious thing about hitting the wall is that it is largely self-induced. In most cases, it can easily be avoided if you prepare for it. You have to have the right nutrition with you on the ride. If I'm on a ride that I know will be longer than 90 minutes, I plan to take in about 100 calories—a gel pack or a large bite of an energy bar—every 30 minutes. And the longer the ride, the more elaborate the plan should be. The point is you must plan it out.

You also have to eat before you feel hungry. There's a lag between the time your body needs the glucose and the time you become aware of the need. By the time you see the symptoms, it's too late—you've already bonked.

On the surface, hitting the wall sounds impressive—almost heroic. But most of the time, we bonk because we haven't planned well or paid attention to our surroundings.

More often than not, it's the uninitiated and undisciplined who bonk.

There's a leadership bonk as well, although the symptoms aren't dizziness, weakness or muscle fatigue. Instead, the symptoms are things like irritability, inflexibility, impatience, poor decision-making, distractibility, a lack of clarity, tunnel-vision, increased stress, lack of forethought, contradiction, reduced memory capacity, sleep disruption and reactive (instead of proactive) behaviors.

Hitting the leadership wall happens when leaders push themselves beyond their available mental, emotional and physical resources. Almost any leadership role (especially in the modern marketplace) will be stressful and challenging, often requiring working longer and harder, which means that bonking could be lurking just around the corner.

You've probably seen the relevant statistics such as:

- 75% of Americans experience symptoms related to stress in a given month, including both physical and psychological symptoms

"If you wait until you see the symptoms, it's too late—you've already bonked."

- One-third of Americans feel they are living with extreme stress
- 48% of Americans claim their stress has increased over the past five years
- Roughly 75% of Americans attribute the leading causes of stress to money and work

What happens in the leadership bonk is complex, but suffice it to say that when you push yourself too hard for too long you'll eventually begin to experience the symptoms described above. At the risk of sounding alarmist, continuing this course will put you into a state of stress that (at the very least) is unhealthy and unproductive and (at the worst) could jeopardize your health—and potentially your career and even your life.

As desperate as this sounds, there's good news. As in cycling, hitting the leadership wall is often self-induced—it can usually be avoided. In his book *Overworked and Overwhelmed: The Mindfulness*

Alternative, executive coach and consultant Scott Eblin describes an alternative to the grinding approach that is all too common in the marketplace today. He describes an intentional, disciplined method for getting out of the state of chronic fight-or-flight response many leaders find themselves in.

At the risk of oversimplifying it, Eblin describes mindfulness as an awareness of how we respond to stimuli and what's happening around us. It's easy to get locked into unthinking, reactionary behaviors that are unproductive or harmful.

Mindfulness might appear abstract and difficult to quantify or apply practically. One of most basic ways I try to practice it is by focusing on two simple metrics: 1) time and 2) thoughts—which you can remember in the formula T^2.

> "It's easy to get locked into unthinking, reactionary behaviors that are unproductive or harmful."

T^1 – Time

Time is more than just "money." It's a resource for your personal sanity! Time provides for the separation you need to get things like ideas, information and perspective on the challenges you face. But you must use it for genuine separation from challenges for it to truly contribute toward mindfulness.

One practical way is by taking what I jokingly call a "walkabout." My coworkers will tell you that, usually once a day in the mid-afternoon, I can be seen walking around the office. It's something I work into my schedule usually when my energy level is waning. A typical walkabout takes about 10-15 minutes, and it's time well spent. When I look at the days I neglect it, it's clear that I can easily waste those minutes in unproductive, grinding work that only leads to "bonking" sooner.

The good thing about time is it's easily measured (both in amount and frequency). The amount of time needed varies with the situation, but it usually doesn't take much. Sometimes, even a few minutes spent intentionally refreshing your thoughts and your attitude will do the trick. Regularity and quality is what you want to aim for.

T² – Thoughts

The second practical mindfulness metric is to be conscious of your thoughts. As I do my walkabout, I force myself to think about something other than the work I'm engaged in. I allow myself to think about almost anything—with only two restrictions: It can't be about work, and it must be positive in nature.

Sometimes, this leads to thoughts about my family; other times, it may be past accomplishments. I'm usually bumping into my coworkers so my thoughts often include them as I inquire about their projects. Sometimes, I don't speak to anyone and simply reflect or pray about whatever comes to mind. Other times, I challenge myself to identify at least one thing that I'm thankful for. I remind myself to think back to my first day at work and how excited I was to start a new job.

> "Waiting to get leadership nutrition almost guarantees a problem. You have to take in resources before you think you need them."

Positive thoughts act as a mental "sorbet," of sorts—cleansing your mental palate and putting you in an objective, productive, refreshed state. Eliminating judgmental, critical, dutiful, heavy or oppressive thoughts puts you in a neutral frame of mind. It doesn't take long to realize that the biggest benefit comes from what you're not thinking about.

As a leader, you need a regular diet of new information, ideas and perspectives. Waiting to get leadership nutrition almost guarantees a problem. You have to take in resources before you think you need them. If you wait until you see the symptoms, it's too late—you've already bonked.

As in cycling, the leadership bonk happens to the uninitiated and undisciplined. Bonking can be overcome, and it's usually not the end of the world. But when it happens, the team and all they're doing will almost surely be impacted.

Set aside the time and consider your thoughts, and feed your leadership what it needs to work correctly.

Put It in Motion

- **You Can—and Will—Bonk if You're Unprepared.** You aren't superhuman, and the rules that govern your physical, emotional and psychological well-being can't be compromised.

- **The Leadership Bonk is Self-Inflicted.** There are exceptions, but most of the time, it happens simply because you allow it to happen. It's a sobering thought, but it also means that it's within your capability to prevent.

- **Measure the Time You Spend Getting Separation From Your Challenges.** Keep track of the amount of time, the time of day/week and frequency spent on refreshing, mindful activities.

- **Be Conscious of Your Thought Patterns.** Be intentional about your thought patterns, steering them toward topics that are positive in nature.

23 – YOU'VE GOT MORE RESOURCES THAN YOU THINK

"The orchestra of one never plays a symphony."
Anonymous

One of the not so obvious things to the casual observer is that well-outfitted riders are clipped to their bike pedals. Cycling shoes have a cleat on the bottom that clips to the pedals in much the same way that a snow skier's boot clips to the skis.

Being firmly attached to the pedals provides some significant advantages. There's a greater sense of control. Clipping in brings an uncanny feeling of being "one" with the bike in a way that's not possible in unclipped pedals. I liken it to the sensation automobile enthusiasts get when they find the perfect tire that makes them feel "one with the road." The crank arms (what the pedals attach to) begin to feel like an extension of your feet as if you grew another joint in your leg. I get better feedback through my feet and I can "read" the pressure I'm applying to the pedal.

Or, maybe it's just that I think I look good in the shoes.

> **"It's not quite doubling your pedaling power— but it's close."**

At any rate, there's one undisputed advantage to clipping in: You get an extra stroke. Normal pedals only allow you to add energy to the bike through pushing on the downstroke. Clipped pedals allow for an upstroke: Pulling up on one pedal as you're pushing down on the other. It's not quite doubling your pedaling power—but it's close.

Another factor is that the two strokes use completely different muscle groups. The downstroke, as you might expect, utilizes the quadriceps muscles on the front of the thigh. The upstroke, however, uses the muscles in the abdominal core, the hamstring muscles in the back of the thigh and different parts of the lower leg. Combining the two strokes together engages all the leg muscles. This brings greater balance and reduces muscle strain from overuse.

The result is that a rider has more resources than may be obvious. It's not uncommon for riders who first graduate to clipped pedals to discover their abdominal core engaging in ways they hadn't previously.

"...leaders today have more access to actionable, informational resources than at any other time in human history."

Of course, having more resources requires that you manage them well. If you're not careful, you can strain the muscles that you haven't previously used. I've discovered muscle groups in my abdomen I never used before, and now I have to stretch them regularly because I overuse them if I'm not careful. Sometimes I find myself getting lazy and overusing the downstroke, or I pull too hard on the upstroke and start cramping. It requires some additional attention and concentration, but once you get the hang of it, you can ride much further and faster for longer periods than you ever could before.

Leaders also have unused, unrealized resources. I'll present three of them for you to consider: 1) a coach, 2) access to tactical and strategic information and 3) your team.

A Coach

Another key leadership resource that is largely underutilized is coaching. Coaching used to be seen as a well-intentioned but largely ineffective, one-off service used only by weak leaders who needed "fixing." Fortunately, the perception of leadership coaching has changed in recent years. Now it's increasingly being viewed as having a strategic advocate and inner-circle relationship that successful leaders depend on for success.

According to the International Coach Federation, a significant number of coaching clients claim improvements in key leadership performance areas as a result of coaching:

- Work performance – 70%
- Business management – 61%
- Time management – 57%
- Team effectiveness – 51%
- Self-confidence – 80%
- Relationships – 73%
- Communication skills – 72%
- Life/work balance – 67%

> "One thing almost all leaders have in common is that there are very few, if any, people they can actually talk to."

Coaching provides leaders with objectivity and perspective they can't get on their own. Each leader must find the coach that fits—it's a relationship after all; it's not one-size-fits-all. The right coach will be a trusted advisor[5], helping you process thoughts and ideas, see patterns and alternatives, gain clarity, confirm priorities, make decisions and implement strategies.

Frankly, leadership is an incredibly isolating role. One thing almost all leaders have in common is that there are very few, if any, people they can actually talk to. Leaders find themselves in an unfortunate Catch-22: They're, simultaneously, part of the team and separate from it. They are responsible for speaking to the team, yet they are limited on what they can say—and how they can say it. They must be close to the team, yet, at the same time, be separate enough to provide accountability and objectivity. Having a good coach in your corner will help you overcome the sense of isolation that comes with this Catch-22.

There are also a number of peer coaching groups available for leaders to join. These groups typically provide outside resources, opportunities for group interaction, support, encouragement and accountability. One of the best group settings I've seen is run by an organization called Vistage. They have groups in most major cities, and they're set up by organization size.

---

[5] Thanks to David Maister, whose book *Trusted Advisor* truly captures the essence of what coaches seek to become for their clients.

Access to Information

I could have just said "the Internet," but access to information is much more than that. I know this has become cliché, but leaders today have more access to actionable, informational resources than at any other time in human history. Let that thought marinate for a second, and then think about the implications. The opportunities we have to access strategic information, leverage networking connections and collaborate with key partners was the stuff of science fiction to leaders a generation ago.

The challenge with abundant information, of course, is that it's abundant. In that sense, information is like water: Without it you can't sustain life, but with too much of it you drown. It's an art to manage and discern:

- How to choose the right—or best—information?
- How to stay abreast of the latest info without drowning in it?
- How to distinguish innovations from fads?
- How much information management should you delegate or outsource, and how much should you process directly?

> "If all of those critical functions are centralized in one person, then the team can't function when something goes sideways..."

This point relates directly with other leadership issues, like burnout (See Chapter 22 – The Wall is Real, and Hitting it Hurts) and decision-making (see Chapter 14 – Decide, Now). Leaders need to make informed decisions so find the balance between not enough and too much information. But most of all, find sources for the right information.

Your Team

The biggest unused resource comes in the form of your team. In most teams, the leader is in control of the team. He/she steers the team, makes the decisions, does the planning, removes the distractions, solves the problems, identifies ways to improve or innovate, etc. The team executes it all.

Meaning: The leader puts himself/herself in the position of being indispensable.

But in cases like this, the leader has also become the choke point. If all of those critical functions are centralized in one person, then the team can't function when something goes sideways—and something always goes sideways. It makes the team extremely inefficient. On top of that, the team members become bored and disengaged. They soon begin to feel like cogs in a wheel—because they are. And the leader ends up doing the bulk of the work.

Not a recipe for success.

Ask yourself this question: "Could this place run without me?" If you got called away, got sick, had another opportunity you couldn't pass up, etc., could you leave without the operation grinding to a halt?

If the answer is "no," then figure out why and what's missing:

- What needs to happen to the people you're directing so they can "run the place?"
- What development do they need?
- Is additional staff necessary?
- Or, maybe, different staff?

> "Ask yourself this question: 'Could this place run without me?'"

Obviously, the leader plays a unique role, and even the best of teams need leadership to function at a high level. But a team that's so dependent on the leader that it cannot function in the leader's absence is not healthy. Asking questions like these shines a light on the holes that need filling and reveals your team's developmental priorities.

If the answer to the "run without me" question is "yes," then you are in a minority. But you're not getting off easy—in fact, your job is probably more challenging. You have to raise the bar on almost everything around you (e.g., the team's purpose and goals, the level of quality, the crispness of execution)—and you have to do it quickly. You run the risk of your team getting bored or complacent. I'm not suggesting making life difficult for them, but you should continue to expand their capability and challenges. Give them more (and more important) things to do, call them to continued excellence and reward them when they achieve it. And, perhaps most challenging of all, you need to continue to develop your leadership ability.

And do it now.

Put It in Motion

- **Leadership is Isolating.** You may find yourself out of ideas and feeling alone as if it's you against the world. It is not.

- **Having a Coach Will Make You a Better Leader.** The right coach will help you think more clearly, plan more effectively and focus on what's most important for you.

- **Today's Leaders Have Access to More Actionable Information than at Any Other Time in Human History.** If you think you're out of ideas or solutions, you're just not trying hard enough.

- **Use Your Team.** Lead and manage the team, but don't get so involved in the operation of the team that you get in their way and become the choke point.

- **Ask Yourself: "Could This Place Run Without Me?"** It's one of the best accountability questions because the answer reveals opportunities to both develop strengths and shore up weaknesses.

---

24 – CRASH AND SKIN BURN

"Success and failure.
We think of them as opposites, but they're really not.
They're companions—the hero and the sidekick."
Laurence Shames

Sometimes, failure in cycling is comical. I remember when I got my first pair of clipped pedals. As I explain in Chapter 23 – You've Got More Resources Than You Think, cycling shoes attach to clipped pedals much in the same way ski boots clip into the bindings of snow skis. You get your foot out by simply turning your heel to the outside. It's easy—*when you remember* to turn your heel to the side.

I remember when Anne, the manager at the Trek Store in St. Pete who sold me the shoes, warned me, "You *will* fall over. It happens to everyone; at some point, it will happen to you too." I went along with it, but on the inside, I knew I wasn't going to approach it the way the average rider would. I would concentrate, think ahead and be ready. And I was true to my word: I didn't fall.

On the first day.

Sure enough, on the second day I fell over at a stoplight. I had unclipped my right foot, preparing to keep my left foot clipped in and put my right foot down. But as I was preparing to stop, I hadn't gotten the weight-shifting thing down, and my center of gravity went left.

> "When riders go down at speed, they go down hard and painfully."

I looked like a goober. You know you look like a goober when people ask from their cars (with a smile on their face), "Are you all right? Do you need any help?"

Yes, I obviously do.

Sometimes, failure in cycling is comical.

Sometimes, unfortunately, failure in cycling can be spectacularly bad. Bone and skin do not mix well with concrete or asphalt at 20 miles per hour. Cyclists often refer to crashing as "going down." When riders go down at speed, they go down hard and painfully. It's chaotic. There's no seatbelt or airbag. Everybody sees it, and it's embarrassing. Expensive bike frames can be trashed. And if the riders are in a tight group, one fall can take out multiple people. It's not a pretty sight.

Failure is all around us. Consider that:
- Two out of five new CEOs and 58% of new executives will fail in the first 18 months
- About half the new businesses will fail before their fourth birthday
- The divorce rate in the U.S. is more than half the rate of marriages

> "After a string of successes, there's nothing healthier than a sober realization that you could have done even better."

Naiveté regarding failure will not position you to successfully lead your organization, group, team or family.

Avoiding Catastrophic Failure

To avoid major failure, you must first recognize that it is, in fact, a real possibility. So the starting place is that you must expect that failure *can* happen to you. Meaning: Don't be stupid; don't believe it will never happen to you because you are in some special class of humanity. This is where humility, collaboration and planning can help you out.

Humility (see Chapter 8) can inoculate us against catching the stupid flu. More often than not, failure comes when you have been basking in the glow of success. As the saying goes, "Pride comes before a fall." There's something about pride that blinds us. But a commitment to improvement and a curiosity that continually asks, "How can I get better?" will help to maintain a humble approach toward your leadership. After a string of successes, there's nothing healthier than a sober realization that you could have done even better.

Collaboration (see Chapter 17 – The Peloton, and Chapter 23 – You've Got More Resources Than You Think) also helps you avoid failure. Having more people in your circle can provide more input and perspectives. Having more "eyes on the target" will increase the probability that problems are seen quicker. This assumes, of course, they have the freedom to speak up and that you trust their input.

When you accept the possibility of failure, you tend to include contingency thinking in your plans. Disciplined leaders include a planning step that leans back to get a good view of the strategy and then looks for how things can go sideways. *What's missing? What assumptions are we making that might be incorrect or incomplete? What could go wrong?*

If you want good results from this step, you must be genuine about it. After all, the question "What could go wrong" can swing both ways. If you don't truly believe that failure is a possibility, you won't see any problems in advance. But if you expect that something could—and very likely will—go wrong, you'll get a much better answer.

Leaders who don't expect failure do not live with the discipline of humility, nor are they willing to give the extra effort required to collaborate. And leaders who lack humility or won't collaborate have—in their minds—already answered the question of what could go wrong: nothing.

> "...leaders who lack humility or won't collaborate have—in their minds—already answered the question of what could go wrong: nothing."

Dealing With Failure

The second thing to emphasize is dealing with failure because—news flash—being human means you will fail at some point. Some failures will be only slightly embarrassing, such as not clipping out at a stop light. In other failures, you go down hard and painfully. They're ungainly and spectacular and usually leave you with a nasty case of skin burn. Everyone sees it, and others can get hurt in the process. It leaves scars.

Hopefully you've done all you can to lead well, and the serious crashes are avoided. But when failure shows up, there are several steps I've found to get through the process in a healthy way.

First, own your part in the event. Acknowledge and take ownership of your actions as well as the assumptions, understanding and decisions that drove them. Deflecting, blaming or excusing—or even denying—does nothing but add to your discredit. And not acknowledging your actions and assumptions keeps you blind to things in your leadership that contributed to the failure. In other words, you're virtually guaranteeing the failure will happen again.

A second step is to commit to transforming yourself. Failure has a way of revealing shortcomings—if you let it. It shines a bright light in what was a dark and hidden room, revealing things you were avoiding—or perhaps never knew were even there. But if you never choose to look in the room, then you'll never truly learn from the failure.

> "Failure ... shines a bright light in what was a dark and hidden room, revealing things you were avoiding—or perhaps never knew were even there."

A third step is to do all you can to repair relationships. Most leadership failures involve other people, and there is likely pain, disappointment and broken trust that must be dealt with. If personal offense has occurred, my counsel is to ask for forgiveness. Embrace and acknowledge that your actions inconvenienced or hurt someone else. You may not be able to completely restore the relationship, but doing what you can allows everyone to move on and make the best of an unfortunate and difficult situation. Hopefully, forgiveness will allow for the offense to be repaired and the relationships to be strengthened.

After taking all of these steps, I encourage you to have a short memory. This is only possible if you have taken the previous steps. But once you've done all you can, there is very little gained from dwelling on it. This only adds to guilt, making you overly self-conscious and reluctant. Guilt is usually a poor motivator (which would be helpful to remember the next time someone you're leading happens to fail). It's good to adopt Ann Landers' perspective, "I'm not a failure. I failed at doing something."

Guilt is a heavy burden you choose to carry; one that always seems to get in the way. It degrades your leadership effectiveness because others will see you behaving as if you have something to prove. You want to remember failures clearly enough to learn a lesson, but beyond that, let it go.

I've only crashed on my bike once (See Chapter 20 – Don't Get Caught Leaning). I was fortunate enough to land on a pile of leaves that spared me from a serious case of road rash. After comically falling over twice at stoplights (I had one more after the one described above), where the only casualty was my pride, I've never even gotten close to a clipped fall again. In each case, I learned from failure. But here's the key: I focus on riding correctly *without dwelling on the fact that I fell.*

> "Guilt, most of the time, is a poor motivator (which would be helpful to remember the next time someone you're leading happens to fail)."

This is a part of living *semper incito*—always forward. I have every expectation not to fail that way again, but I ride with the healthy realization that I could— and will, if I don't take steps to ride properly. It's riding with my eyes wide open: Knowing the risks and preparing for what could happen. Through intention and preparation, I'm free to enjoy the benefits that riding brings.

I don't live in fear of repeating missteps in the past; I live in the freedom of purposeful action moving forward. I can only achieve this when I take Werner Erhard's words to heart, "Create your future from your future, not your past."

I've failed in previous leadership roles. Some were embarrassing and unfortunate, but no one was hurt. In other cases, people were genuinely offended and disappointed. The steps above have helped me improve as a leader, though I have so much further to go. And though I have further to go, my failures have prepared me to avoid them from happening again.

Semper incito.

Put It in Motion

- **Confidence is a Leadership Asset.** But overconfidence can blind you to the prospect of failure. If you're an uber-confident leader, you would do well to genuinely accept that failure can happen to you.

- **Stay Relentlessly Curious About Your Own Development.** Regularly ask yourself, "How can I get better?" If you're honest about the question and you listen well to the answer, you'll stay humble about your success.

- **Use Trusted Advisors.** Get perspective on issues from people you trust, who will often see things you may not.

- **Add Contingency Planning to Your Strategies.** Be serious about considering alternative plans if things don't go as planned.

- **Deal With Failures When They Happen.** Own and accept your role in the process, look at transforming yourself where necessary and restore damaged relationships where appropriate.

- **Keep a Short Memory.** Once you've done all you possibly can to deal with the results of failure, clear your conscience and move on. Dwelling on it and using guilt as motivation is rarely effective.

- **Remember: We Usually Grow More From Failure Than From Success.** If When you fail, look for how to improve from it.

25 – THE FASTER YOU CAN *GO*, THE FASTER YOU *CAN* GO

"I wasted time, and now doth time waste me."
Shakespeare

You expend a lot of energy in cycling. A 30-mile ride averaging 20 mph will burn about 2000 calories. When you burn this much energy you develop a keen awareness of efficiency. You want to get the most out of every effort because even a very slight gain in efficiency becomes significant when it's multiplied by thousands of pedal strokes, resulting in huge gains. As I discuss in Chapter 9 – By the Sweat of Your Brow, in cycling, efficiency is king.

This means things such as keeping your upper body still; any side-to-side movement is wasted energy that could be channeled into the pedals. It also means not using muscles that don't contribute to the cycling stroke (your lower back muscles, for example).

But the greatest gain in efficiency comes from being in the right gear. If you're in a gear that's too high for your current speed and road grade, you end up pushing harder to get through the stroke. If you're in a gear that's too low, you spin the pedal around with ease but the lack of resistance means you haven't moved the bike forward. Either way, you burn energy that doesn't translate into forward momentum.

> "When you're in the right gear with decent speed and a high cadence, the increased efficiency means that you are able to go faster…"

Not good.

Enter the measurement of cadence. Cadence is the speed of your pedal stroke in revolutions per minute. Each cyclist has a cadence "sweet zone." While this zone varies with each individual cyclist and their body makeup, keeping your cadence somewhere between 87-100 rpm will ensure your pedal strokes will give you the highest output at the lowest possible energy expended.

To beginning riders this can feel abnormally fast. The comfortable cadence is probably in the mid 70's to the mid 80's so mid 90's seems excessive at first. But just a little bit of practice and experimentation with the higher range soon wins the day. It takes some concentration and practice of watching the cadence reading on your trip computer and knowing which gear to be in for a given situation. You can quickly get comfortable riding in this range.

This sounds like a yogism, but in cycling, going faster lets you go faster. When you're in the right gear with decent speed and a high cadence, the increased efficiency means you are able to go faster—with greater consistency and for longer periods of time. The faster you can *go*, the faster you *can* go.

> "As a leader, speed is often—though not always—an asset. But efficiency absolutely is."

In leadership, the point is not (necessarily) to go faster. As a leader, speed is often—though not always—an asset. But efficiency absolutely is. Efficiency in the leadership stroke is what you're looking for because it's so easy to expend energies that don't move you forward. All your practice, discipline, training and execution need to be as efficient as possible. You need to get the most out of every conversation, every strategy, every directive, every meeting.

Here are a few areas you can practice on to improve the efficiency of your leadership stroke:

Delegating

Taking on too much is a sure way to dilute your energies and decrease your efficiency. Don't exert more energy on things than you have to. Offload things that slow you down (and that other people on your team do better than you).

Delegating is a much broader discipline than simply dumping your work onto someone else. Delegation is about the development of your team and leveraging the reality that teams outperform individuals. But I include it here because one of the realities about leaders who are poor delegators is they struggle giving away responsibility.

Sometimes it's because leaders feel that no one else can perform the task as well as they can. Other times it's because the leader enjoys the work. Other times it's that they don't trust their team to get the work done.

Whatever the reason, understand this: If you don't delegate, your only alternative is to micromanage. If that's as distasteful to you as I hope it is, then you'll commit to become a collaborative leader: co-laboring with others as you influence them to get things done. You will soon get comfortable with it as you begin to realize that delegating is a much more sound, profound, energizing, empowering and effective approach to take.

> "If you don't delegate, your only alternative is to micromanage."

Thinking

Don't overthink. You certainly don't want to under think or ignore the details, but you should get increasingly comfortable picking up the pace of your analysis, evaluation and decision-making processes. This will be truer for those leaders who are naturally process-oriented thinkers.

Communicating

Review your communications to find ways to be more efficient. Be clear, be concise. As the presentation saying goes, "Be brilliant. Be brief. Be gone."

Be as succinct as possible, without compromising what people understand. Make your statements as brief as you can, yet communicate enough that people have fully understood your message.

Did you catch that I repeated myself? Isn't it kind of boring—maybe even frustrating—to hear the same thing over and over again, unnecessarily?

Focusing

Don't allow yourself to get distracted. Focusing on priorities will help to keep your energy targeted and efficient. Periodically, look at your task list and decide what you're going to let go of. Rare is the day we end up with free time and nothing to work on. More often than not, we acquire extra stuff to do, whether we have time for it or not. As Peter Drucker aptly observed, "There is nothing so useless as doing efficiently that which should not be done at all."

> "There is nothing so useless as doing efficiently that which should not be done at all."
>
> *Peter Drucker*

Lee Iacocca's adage, "The speed of the boss is the speed of the team," is usually thought of in terms of driving for results. But you could make a parallel expression for efficiency: "The *manner* of speed of the leader is the *manner* of speed of the team." Meaning: How a leader maintains speed will affect how the team maintains speed. A leader's efficiency doesn't guarantee the team's efficiency, but a leader's inefficiency usually guarantees inefficiency on the part of the team.

For any leader with a naturally slower cadence, this higher manner-of-speed-of-the-leader cadence will likely feel excessively fast. But with some deliberate practice, it will quickly become comfortable, and you'll find yourself going faster.

Put It in Motion

- **Speed Might Be an Asset, But Efficiency Always Is.** Efficiency keeps you from wasting energy and resources no matter how fast you're trying to go.

- **If You Don't Delegate, You'll Never Lead Efficiently.** Without delegation, you end up doing double the work: yours and your team's. Eventually, you'll burn out, and your team will get frustrated by your micromanagement.

- **Don't Overthink.** Disciplining yourself to pick up the cadence of your analysis and decision-making will allow you to get to decision points and execution sooner.

- **Communicate Efficiently.** I'm not suggesting you limit your communication to 140 characters or less. But you should avoid getting on soapboxes, showing off your knowledge or overdoing it when giving your opinion. Try to say it in as few words as necessary to ensure clarity and understanding.

- **A Lack of Focus Almost Always Means a Lack of Efficiency.** Not focusing leads to spending energy on unnecessary things.

- **Leadership Efficiency is About Maintaining Speed.** The less energy required to keep moving the team forward the better.

26 – RIDING THE THIN LINE

"In the long run, men hit only what they aim at."
Henry David Thoreau

Sometimes a subtle shift in perspective changes everything.

Staying in line is a riding discipline. To ride predictably and with stability is a good thing. I like it when my wheels go where I want them to go.

So early on I started trying to ride on the two-inch line that separates the bike lane from automobile traffic. I wanted to be able to ride the line without falling off. It's hard to do for extended periods of time. There are a lot of things that distract you and pull you away from where you want to go. I was not very good at it, and I repeatedly got wobbly, crisscrossing over and back and forth.

One day, after struggling again to ride on the line, I discovered a very subtle—but vital—shift in thinking that changed everything for me. Instead of trying not to miss the line, I tried to hit it. Focusing on the target brought my balance back and allowed me to ride the thin line for long sections at a time.

> "With my gaze fixed on where I'm going, my wheels simply follow along."

There are two dynamics at work here.

One is a change of perspective. Trying not to miss the line makes me shortsighted. My eyes almost always focus on the line immediately in front of the wheel.

But in shifting my mindset to hit the line, my eyes instinctively look up—out in front. The new perspective forces me to think forward, to see where the line is going. With my gaze fixed on where I'm going, my wheels simply follow along. I don't have to worry as much about what is right in front of my wheel.

The second dynamic is the result of a focused mind. Or to state it differently: removing the clutter of a conflicted mind. Trying not to fall off the line is reactive and defensive. In contrast, hitting the line is proactive, creating a natural clarity that puts you in control of your own environment.

You can see how the two dynamics work together. Focusing on the short-term and the immediate creates reactions to stimuli or events that, when it's all said and done, are unimportant and incompatible with the direction you want to go. There will always be things that work to pull you off the line you want to take. There will always be crosswinds, obstacles and gaps in the pavement. Sometimes the line will be unclear, and sometimes it will disappear altogether. If you focus strictly on what's right in front of you, along with the distractions and the many ways you *can* fail, more often than not you *will* fail.[6]

> "There is a huge difference between trying to succeed and trying not to fail."

There's a huge difference between trying to succeed and trying not to fail. There are many ways to fall off your line. But there are only a few things you must do stay on target. In trying not to fail, your target is failure. In trying to succeed, your target is success.

The principle is the same, whether the focus is success or failure: You hit what you aim for.

This is where vision comes into play. Being visionary means that you can see the line further out than most people, beyond the typical and ordinary roads that have already been ridden. Indeed, it may mean you can see roads and lines that don't even exist.

People respond and commit to a compelling vision, a grand adventure or a noble cause. Depending on the situation, people will make personal sacrifices to help vision become reality. At many points in history people have—literally—given their lives for a worthy vision.

---

[6] Incidentally, some will restate this principle of focus as "Don't get caught up in the details." But that statement should be used with caution. Leaders *need* to pay attention to details because some of them are important. The key is to make sure you're paying attention to the right details—and not getting distracted by the wrong ones.

But there's a difference between *having* a vision and *accomplishing* a vision. Anyone with the ability to dream has a vision. It's quite another thing to maintain the focus on proper execution. There's a distinction between being a visionary and being a visionary leader. Both can anticipate a potential future, see where the line goes and even understand how it progresses from here to there. But it takes a skillful leader to keep the organization on-line, to know which details to focus on and which stimuli to reject.

This is where the best visionary leaders shine brightly, as a lighthouse in a storm. They're able to keep their team from being distracted by stuff that pulls them off-line—things that are urgent, beneficial and even enticing but are only distractions in the context of fulfilling the vision. It's equal parts inspiration and execution, skillfully combined.

> "...it takes a skillful leader to keep the organization on-line, to know which details to focus on and which stimuli to reject."

In your leadership, do you ever find yourself trying not to fail? Playing it safe so as not to mess up or aiming for the minimum level of exposure and risk? Do you find your team distracted, captivated or distressed about all the ways things could go wrong? Do you find them becoming reluctant or hesitant? Are they getting pulled into things that have more urgency than importance?

If so, shift your and your team's perspective and focus on the success that's waiting out in front of you.

Making a shift in perspective changes everything.

143

Put It in Motion

- **Spend More Time Looking Further Out Front.** Focusing primarily on the immediate makes you lose sight of where you want to go.

- **You Hit What You Aim For.** In trying not to fail, your target is failure. In trying to succeed, your target is success.

- **Trying Not to Fail is Distracting.** There are often so many ways to fail and only a few ways to succeed. If you approach success by trying not to fail, you'll almost certainly be distracted from success.

- **Trying Not to Fail Makes You Reactive and Defensive.** Trying to succeed keeps you in a proactive mindset and removes the distractions that clutter your thinking.

- **There Will Always be Distractions.** Looking beyond the immediate will help you see problems and hazards sooner, and you can still keep what's immediately in front of you in your peripheral vision.

- **People Need a Vision.** They—and you—need to know the big picture, the ultimate destination. It brings energy and clarity.

- **There's a Difference Between a Visionary and a Visionary Leader.** Lots of people can envision a better future. It takes leadership to keep the team online, undistracted and executing to achieve a better future. It's equal parts inspiration and execution, skillfully combined.

27 – NEGOTIATE THE CURVES

"In order to win a man to your cause, you must first reach his heart, the great high road to his reason."
Abraham Lincoln

I am, admittedly, a "flatlander."

Riding in Florida means most of my rides are on straight, level roads. When I do get the rare chance to get into the hills, it's a whole new experience. In many ways, it's like learning to ride all over again.

Curves add an extra dimension to riding. Curves require you to bank and turn and apply extra pressure to the handlebars. You're shifting your weight, which changes your center of gravity and affects your rate of turn. If you add elevation changes to the mix, you're now accelerating or decelerating at the same time you're turning. This means the stability of the bike changes, and you must pay attention to every input into the bike: steering, leaning, braking and pedaling.

> **"Do you really want to be out of position when the landscape of your ride changes?"**

What you see in front of you changes quickly. Unexpected objects and road hazards may come without warning, and you must be prepared to adapt even as you're dealing with the turns.

In short, everything you do on straight, flat roads you must also do on the curves, except more purposefully. It's more complicated and requires an extra level of attention. You must manage yourself and the bike. You must negotiate them.

Of course, you could choose to dismiss the need for this skill of negotiating the curves. It may seem unnecessary, like it's overthinking things. You could see a curve as something that gets you to the next straightaway—because the straightaway is where most of the action occurs.

You could just ignore the challenge curves bring. You could take your best shot, make the most of it and just get through the turns as they come. It's not like every curve you encounter is going to be a life-or-death issue.

But anyone who races anything (except drag racers) will tell you that pushing on the accelerator and going fast in the straightaway is the easy part. Racers make their living and their legacy in how they handle the curves. And think of it this way: Do you really want to be out of position when the landscape of your ride changes? Do you really want to just wing it, hope for the best?

I don't and prefer to develop the extra skill as I have opportunity to. Frankly, riding the curves is so much more fun.

Besides, there's one thing I've learned: If you can negotiate the curves, going straight is a piece of cake.

> "If you can negotiate the curves, going straight is a piece of cake."

There's a leadership behavior that equates to riding the curves, one that's unique from almost every other behavior. Leaders that exhibit this extra behavior are winsome in a way that attracts other people and builds a deeper level of trust and engagement. They're endearing; they're able to produce higher levels of commitment to the cause. There are many expressions of this behavior, but for simplicity's sake, I'll call it persuasion.

Persuasion allows you to work *with* others instead of simply making demands *of* others. Leaders who exercise this competency have the ability to navigate the politics of an organization. They can recognize the subtle differences between groups, departments or divisions. They have an understanding about the culture of the organization, what is truly valued and how decisions are made. They know just what to say, and they say it in a way that doesn't offend or demean others. They have a sixth sense about how to navigate the greys of an organization instead of seeing things always as black or white. They're flexible enough to involve the passions and perspectives of all parties instead of creating my-way-or-the-highway ultimatums. And they do so in a way that does more than merely leverage people. Instead, they are able to unify people.

By using the word "persuasion" in this chapter, I don't mean to oversimplify it to "getting what you want." Instead, I'm lumping together all of the behaviors that relate to mastering relationships and the art of understanding people and working with them. Things like:

- Identifying and empathizing with others
- Appreciating others and their positions, concerns and interests
- Listening well
- Having political savvy
- Creating consensus
- Moving people to embrace new ideas
- Engaging others to act when they're hesitant or reluctant
- Developing trust
- Eliminating skepticism
- Convincing others
- Resolving conflicts
- Speaking to people's hearts, not just their heads
- Being engaging, winsome

> "Persuasion allows you to work *with* others instead of simply making demands *of* others."

I suspect these are the things some people have in mind when they refer to leadership "soft skills"—a moniker I've come to detest. "Soft" can imply these behaviors are secondary, as if to say they're not really required but a plus if you have them.

Frankly, I've found it's the other way around. Leaders who exhibit these behaviors separate themselves from the pack. Leaders who can influence people by working with them instead of simply directing them are ultimately the most effective.

"Soft" may also imply these behaviors are easy to learn. In fact, they are hard to learn. It takes more attention to detail to be a persuasive leader. It takes more intentionality. And it takes more self-awareness. These are not items you check off a to-do list; they're behaviors you have to practice—and practice deliberately— if you want to master them (see Chapter 16 – Practice Doesn't Make Perfect).

Remember, working with people can be as much art as science. Because they're human, people have good and bad days. They fluctuate. The landscape of their productivity is constantly changing. They have their own priorities and goals. They have hopes. They have fears; so they feel threatened at times and get protective and defensive. They want to belong; to play a role. They have history and personal values. All of these must be taken into account if you truly want to get the best out of people.

> "It all hinges on this reality: Leaders lead *people*. Not strategies, or processes, or ideas or things. *People*."

It all hinges on this reality: Leaders lead *people*. Not strategies, or processes, or ideas or things. *People*.

If you can't work with *people*, what *are* you going to work with?

If you can't work *with* people, what are you going to do when you discover you are working *against* them?

Leaders who are competent at working with people are capable at other leadership behaviors, too, like the ability to give direction or make decisions. But they have added persuasive behaviors. They know almost any quality leader can do things like give direction or make decisions. Those things are like being a flatlander: pushing straight ahead, without concern for the curvy environment of relationships that will ultimately determine success.

They know that, ultimately, negotiating the curves is so much more fun.

And they know if they can negotiate the curves, leading when the road is straight is a piece of cake.

Put It in Motion

- **If You Can Work Well With People, The Other Aspects of Leadership Are Easy.** The "soft" skills are the hard part. Mastering these will make every other part of leading so much easier.

- **Leaders Lead *People*.** Not strategies, or processes, or ideas or things. *People.* If you can't work with people, what are you going to work with?

- **Don't Let Poor Interactive Behaviors Undermine Your Leadership.** If you can't work *with* people, what are you going to do when you discover you are working *against* them?

28 – BE AFRAID, BUT NOT VERY AFRAID

"Here is the world.
Beautiful and terrible things will happen.
Don't be afraid."
Frederick Buechner

I was a good athlete in my younger years, though I was never imposing. At five feet, seven inches tall, I weighed in at 145 pounds. I was always playing against bigger guys in football and basketball, and I doubt I ever intimidated any of them.

I was, however, strong for my size. I've done my fair share of weightlifting and could bench-press over 200 pounds and squat 370 pounds as a high school sophomore. I could easily exceed 100 push-ups and 50 pull-ups. I got into cheerleading at the University of Arkansas and started doing some gymnastics moves: back flips, back handsprings, etc., as well as having people stand on my shoulders in pyramids. It was all great fun, and I have some wonderful memories.

"For me, it came in a willful conviction... I will no longer allow fear to command me."

Now, as a member of the half-century club, my body is paying for it. I've got the usual aches and issues my age group deals with, but the biggest payment I make is dealing with the damage to my spine. I've had two surgeries to repair herniated discs, one in my lower back and one in my neck—with another possible neck surgery looming in the future. My discs have compressed to the point that I've lost a full inch in height. If I hold my head in the wrong position while typing this manuscript, my left arm starts complaining.

For a year leading up to my neck surgery, the pain was unrelenting. There's nothing quite like the pain of an impinged nerve. The closest way to describe it is a burning sensation, something like the ache you feel after you've touched a hot stove. Except it's not on the skin, it's deep inside. I could feel it running the length of my arm. My thumb, index and middle fingers all went numb. I had that pins-and-needles feeling (like when your foot goes to sleep) in my hand and forearm all the time; it never went away.

The constancy of nerve pain is the most difficult part. Medication is largely ineffective. It's inescapable; it's exhausting, but you can't sleep. No position is comfortable for long; you toss and turn until you get up because you can't lie there any longer. It monopolizes your life and your thoughts. You become imprisoned in the pain as it presses in on all sides. It takes all you've got to not let pain define you.

> "Courage is resistance to fear, mastery of fear, not absence of fear."
>
> *Mark Twain*

I got my first bike, the Beast (see Chapter 1 – Go With What You've Got), as a gift from my brother-in-law long before my neck surgery. I didn't ride the bike for a few years, in part because leaning over the handlebars in the riding position with my neck issues was not doable.

After my surgery I faced a big decision. I finally had relief from the pain—a new lease on life—so I didn't want to risk anything that would cause another injury. Yet not exercising almost guaranteed my body would deteriorate, and the pain would return. The prospect of facing that level of pain again was genuinely frightening ... in ways I couldn't describe to others nor, frankly, even to myself. It seemed like the risk was worth it so I took it.

Am I ever glad I did.

Riding ended up being the perfect exercise for strengthening the muscles in my neck and back. The proper riding position also moves the chest forward, holds the head in line with the spine and engages the abdominal core. I now have better posture than ever before.

Riding, in a very real sense, gave me life—a life I would not have had if fear had its way with me.

Fear is one of the first things you should deal with when you consider what kind of a leader you want to be. How you will handle fear and the role you allow it to play will impact your leadership performance in significant ways.

At the risk of sounding like an overgeneralization, consider these aspects of leadership and how fear can shape them in a negative way (stay with me):

- Your thoughts, what you focus on and consider
- Your self-perception
- Your vision of the future
- Your decision-making
- Your objectivity
- Your optimism
- Your perception of reality
- Your level of engagement
- Your perception about other people, their abilities and their motives
- Your level of collaboration with others
- How you treat other people
- Your comfort level with risk
- The pace and scope of your work
- Your effectiveness at exercising *authority*—instead of *power*
- Your ability to be "whole" and to be balanced between work and the rest of your life
- Your ability to forgive others
- Your resiliency and how you respond to disappointment and setback
- Your tolerance for mistakes and failure—your own as well as others'
- Your ability to trust other people and to be transparent with them
- Your effectiveness as a team member
- Your communication effectiveness
- Your agility and adaptability

> "Fear—or better said how you *manage* fear—will impact the effectiveness of your leadership in virtually everything you do."

I could go on. But I hope you get the picture. Fear—or better said how you *manage* fear—will impact the effectiveness of your leadership in virtually everything you do.

This topic could be a book all by itself. In an attempt to stay practical, I'm taking a high-level view of fear and how it affects leadership by answering two basic questions:

1. What is there to be afraid of?
2. What do I do about it?

What is There to be Afraid of?

There are two broad categories of fear that frequently come into play for leaders: loss of status and interpersonal fears.

Fears related to the loss of status encompass anything that threatens our current role. It could be losing our position (e.g., a job, a role, a function within a group or organization). It could be losing the regard of others. In short, it's natural to fear anything that threatens the safety and security we prefer.

> "...leadership involves relationships with other people. You'll achieve your highest level of influence with people when you can relate with them."

Managing this type of fear is a matter of how big we allow the fear to be and how we choose to respond to it. For instance, we face losing our job if we fail to grow our skill sets. We can choose to respond in a productive way with healthy patterns of self-improvement, or we can respond with paranoid, attacking, defensive behaviors that diminish our effectiveness. Perhaps the best news is that there is a choice. Often, we feel driven into unhealthy patterns—but we don't have to be.

Interpersonal fear shows up in how we interact with others. Some people fear confrontation. Others fear intimacy or transparency. Many fear a loss of control or domination. Still others fear disappointing or failing others.

Many of the dynamics that create this fear come from years of interacting with people. We have been shaped—powerfully and profoundly—by experience and our environment; sometimes this shaping was gradual and subtle. Other times it was sudden and traumatic. Unless we've probed and researched it, most of us have little awareness of the ways we've been shaped.

At issue is the inescapable reality that leadership involves relationships with other people. You'll achieve your highest level of influence with people when you can relate with them. And if interpersonal fears preside in your interactions with other people, the quality of your relationships will suffer. Fear puts you into a self-preservation mindset rather than a service mindset. You can't influence—or develop—someone as effectively if you're primarily protecting your own interests and dominating the interaction.

It's rare to find a leader who's learned to manage interpersonal fears well. It takes effort and a willingness to be introspective that, frankly, most leaders don't have time for—either because they can't or won't take the time.

How much is it affecting you? That is a question only you can answer. And you'll never answer it until you ask it. Oftentimes, this is the hardest part. Once you do, if you're honest with yourself and you keep digging, you'll most likely find the answer.

> "It's rare to find a leader who's learned to manage interpersonal fears well."

What Do I Do About It?

Three steps must be taken if you want to avoid being very afraid:
- Recognize fear
- Face fear
- Take back fear's authority

Recognize Fear

All of us are afraid of something. Having some level of fear doesn't make you weak, it makes you human. So the first step in dealing with fear is to recognize and admit it is there and to be aware of how it affects you.

Some people take the "ignorance is bliss" approach. They avoid fear; they prefer to remain unaware, to keep it invisible.

Perhaps they've never thought about it—or perhaps they refused to think about it.

For others, fear is a present reality. They are very much aware of the things that frighten them (though they may not admit it to others). They try to stay one step ahead of it or keep it hidden in the closet.

Either way, the practical result is largely the same: We're blind to fear. It influences our actions, but we don't (or won't) see it. Unknowingly, we try to compensate. It's the compensation that throws us off track.

Sometimes (particularly early in our formation as leaders) this compensation can help our cause and may lead to some initial leadership success. Avoiding fear can look like bravado[7]. Staying one step ahead of fear can mimic tireless devotion, taking initiative or adapting quickly to change. This initial success makes it harder to face fear in the end because it rewards the wrong behaviors.

> "Having some level of fear doesn't make you weak, it makes you human."

Eventually, our compensation weakens our effectiveness. Maintaining compensating behaviors becomes a higher priority than displaying the leadership behavior that's right for the challenge. And as our leadership responsibilities grow or when we face a leadership crisis, our behavior comes off as odd or misplaced; our decisions can have that out-of-the-blue quality. Conversations can seem out of touch.

That's because we're not responding to the current environment, we're responding to fear. And sooner or later, others will see it. Depending on how good you are at suppressing or covering up your fear, they may not recognize that fear drove your behavior, but they'll see your behavior and disengage, lose trust, pull back or any of a host of other responses—none of which are productive.

---

[7] Of course, it's an oversimplification to assume that any or all bravado is based in fear. Don't fall into that trap.

Face Fear

Until we are willing to face fear, it always remains hidden, in the dark, hiding in the bushes. By default our compensating (at the very least) gives it validity and (at worst) gives it power. In its mystery, it remains formidable. And it *will* impact what we do.

So, at some point—if you don't want it to command your leadership—you must face fear. Let me explain what I mean.

I'm not suggesting you should dwell on it. Facing fear doesn't involve making it so much a part of your conscious thought that it becomes a part of every conversation or every decision.

Instead, facing fear comes in simple recognition.

Obviously, this will look different for every individual. But success in facing fear comes in recognizing it's real and understanding how it impacts you. 90% of the battle is simply facing that fact. Once faced, fear becomes much less potent.

As Franklin Roosevelt famously put it, "The only thing we have to fear is fear itself."

> "Until we are willing to face fear, it always remains hidden, in the dark, hiding in the bushes ... And it *will* impact what we do."

One of my favorite movie scenes depicting a leader facing his fear is from Mel Gibson's *Braveheart*. Robert the Bruce (played by Angus Macfadyen) was afraid of losing his title as heir to the throne of Scotland. Fed by his father's controlling and self-interested insecurities, the Bruce was indecisive, hedging and hesitant to take a stand. Hiding behind his role as the future king of Scotland, he was unable to project vision, confidence or influence. In short, he had the title but was ineffective as a leader.

You can see the awareness in the Bruce's eyes as the light bulb turns on: "Men don't follow titles," says Wallace/Gibson, "They follow courage."

Take Away Fear's Control

Fear does have a place as a motivator, but it's important to not give it a controlling interest. This requires the active step of seizing control of your response. This sounds simple enough but, in fact, takes courage—the leader's appropriate response to fear. As Mark Twain said, "Courage is resistance to fear, mastery of fear, not absence of fear." Simply put, courage is action by choice not by compulsion. In the leadership context, it means recognizing the reality of the thing(s) that frightens us and the potential consequences and willfully choosing to act in spite of that fear.

This is, I believe, the most powerful and compelling aspect of managing fear. It comes with practice. The more you do it the better you'll get at it. Start slow and start early. The earlier you can develop courage in your leadership, the sooner you'll develop the practice and discipline. You'll create new habits, and you'll start to recognize the degree to which you've allowed fear to hold sway over you.

And you will master it.

> "...courage is action by choice not by compulsion."

For me, it came in a willful conviction. It was a practical, psychological, emotional and very much a spiritual decision. At the time—somewhat naively—I made the stated declaration that I was no longer going to be afraid of anything. Time and experience have translated that declaration into a more proper and practical position: I will no longer allow fear to command me.

What it will look like for you is up to you. It's your choice so you must take ownership of it.

My encouragement to you is simply this: Be afraid; just don't allow yourself to be very afraid.

Put It in Motion

- **Deal With Fear First.** It's one of the first issues you should address because it can affect human behavior so profoundly. How you manage fear will impact the effectiveness of your leadership in virtually everything you do.

- **Fear Puts You in the Wrong Mindset.** Fear puts you into a self-preservation mindset rather than a service mindset. You can't influence someone as effectively if you're primarily protecting your own interests.

- **Recognize Your Fears and the Ways You Compensate for Them.** You're probably not aware of how you're reacting to your fears. Fear introduces compensating behaviors that often don't match the current environment, and they can cause others to lose trust in you.

- **Facing Fear Removes its Power.** Like Franklin Roosevelt said, "The only thing we have to fear is fear itself."

- **Take Away Fear's Control by Resisting It.** "Courage is resistance to fear, mastery of fear, not absence of fear," said Mark Twain. Courage is recognizing the reality of the thing(s) that frightens us and willfully choosing to act in spite of the influence of that fear.

29 – ENDURE

"What is harder than rock, or softer than water?
Yet soft water hollows out hard rock.
Persevere."
Ovid

I remember my first ride on my original bike, "The Beast." The ride itself was not so remarkable. But the effect on my legs was: After the ride, they didn't want to work. Bending my knees for the first few minutes after getting off the bike was like being the Tin Man after a rainstorm. It was as if I had pipes for legs and walking was more shuffling than anything else. I could get into a chair without incident but getting out of it was another story. It was this way for the next day or so as I shouldered the embarrassment of being so out of shape.

I had the same experience several times over the next few rides as each time I increased the length or pace of my rides. But after that, going faster and further didn't really affect my legs any more. I thought it an accomplishment that my legs were in shape and that I'd established myself as a cyclist.

> "...endurance is measured over time in sustained, consistent execution."

Then I went on my first "long" ride (described in Chapter 8 – Humility). This ride revealed I had much further to go. It opened a window of awareness that serious riding is an all-in proposition: It requires your whole body to be in shape, not just your legs. I understood my weakness was not my lack of leg strength. It was my lack of endurance.

Riding calls louder for endurance than for strength. Endurance is about exertion over the long haul. It requires a holistic commitment, not just a partial investment.

Endurance is a completely different focus compared to strength. Strength is a momentary, single-point exertion that you may only have to demonstrate once. But endurance is measured over time in sustained, consistent execution. Strength gets revealed through overcoming a specific challenge, while endurance gets revealed through finishing the race.

Subsequently longer rides showed that the investment of strength in my legs paid off. Once I developed an initial level of strength, even going on a 70-mile ride didn't seriously challenge my legs. But it did challenge my endurance.

> "One of the questions about leadership I hear most often is the age-old, 'Are leaders born or made?'"

Similarly, leadership excellence is measured in terms of consistent execution over time. It's (relatively speaking) easy to be a rock star for short bursts, to get one gutsy prediction right, to make a few good decisions in a row or to push through one barrier to success.

But it's quite another to string together months and years of sustained leadership success. Leadership is a marathon, where the real victory comes in finishing. You don't finish by running fast. You finish by running far. You must develop endurance—*develop* being the key word.

One of the questions about leadership I hear most often is the age-old, "Are leaders born or made?" It's a great question, to which my answer is, "Yes"—it's both. Some people are born with certain qualities—things like temperament and personality—that position them as natural leaders. On top of that, experiences in their life give them an advantage when it comes to being a leader such as parenting, nurturing, background, experience or their network of associates or mentors. All of these can be leveraged for leadership success.

But these qualities are analogous to strength. They are an advantage, but they aren't the secret sauce. They must be appropriately applied and leveraged *over time*. It takes practice to know when and how best to deploy them.

In fact, it's not uncommon for leadership failure to come from overreliance on natural qualities. Because these qualities have helped them in the past, leaders don't develop the other competencies—they become a "one-trick pony" so to speak. And because these qualities are "natural," leaders aren't even aware they have them and fail to understand how the qualities can be leveraged. And when the circumstances get more complex or the scope of responsibility broadens, leaders discover they are unable to simply "muscle through" the circumstances. Leaders must shift their mindset so they become aware of the need to develop endurance for the long ride—not just strength for the short ride.

Abraham Lincoln was one such leader. Regarding his political career, it's been said that he failed himself into the presidency—that he hung around long enough to finally become president. While that assessment is somewhat simplistic, it is clear that his leadership is characterized by endurance. Contrast the results of Lincoln's time in the White House with almost any other president who rose quickly to become the chief executive of the government of the United States, and you'll see the results of sustained execution over time.

> "...it's not uncommon for leadership failure to come from overreliance on natural qualities."

Lincoln was not privileged or naturally well-qualified. His early years were probably best characterized as survival as he and his family had to forge an existence in the frontier. His younger brother died as an infant, and his mother died when he was nine years old.

He was largely self-educated; it's estimated he only had a total of 18 months of formal education in his entire life. He fed his natural curiosity, which led to a tenacious attitude toward learning. He was a voracious reader and often read books multiple times because they were the only ones available to read.

He eventually became a shop-keeper and postmaster, which is likely where he honed his political savvy and his ability to read and understand people. He learned to apply his wit and personality in a way that endeared people to him. He then became a lawyer, and his years in the practice were characterized by fairness, consistency and a piercing clarity of thought.

His outward appearance did him no political favors. He looked the part of a backwoodsman. He was tall at six foot four inches and very thin. He had a plopping, long-strided gait, one that communicated anything but grace and polish. He also had a high-pitched voice in sharp contrast with the natural booming voice of the orators of his time. No doubt his legal and political opponents underestimated him.

Upon winning the presidency, he deviated from the political norm by selecting his greatest political opponents to join his cabinet. He was long-suffering with his detractors, habitually choosing grace over punishment when his cabinet members and military generals undermined his initiatives and openly worked against him—sometimes to the extreme of taking the blame for their misdeeds, divisive attitudes and otherwise insubordinate behavior. His influence over these men changed them from fierce opponents to close, personal friends and allies by the time of his assassination.

He is widely regarded by most as one of the most effective presidents the United States has ever produced, who governed during one of the most trying seasons of our nation's history.

Lincoln endured.

Put It in Motion

- **The True Leadership Challenge Requires Endurance.** It's relatively easy to have leadership success once. It's quite another to succeed consistently over time. The best leaders display patterns of excellence over varied circumstances and environments, and this requires endurance.

- **Endurance Results From Developing Natural Qualities.** The more aware of your natural leadership qualities you are, the more equipped you are to leverage them over time in varied situations.

30 – ENJOY THE RIDE

"Keep it simple, follow your gut,
listen to advice from people you trust—
and keep smiling."
Anthony Hyde

It was the day after Christmas. It'd been a difficult year from a work standpoint. I'd had limited time off, and I'd worked more weekends than I care to admit. The point is: For some time, I'd been looking forward to taking off the week between Christmas and New Year's Day so I could catch up on riding my bike. The plan was to ride each day, getting some extended time to increase the length of my rides. And I'd truly been looking forward to it more than Christmas itself.

But on Christmas Eve, I strained my ankle. I was having trouble walking on it by the end of the day. I iced it quickly, and by the end of the following day—Christmas Day—I was able to walk largely pain free, but it still hurt to move it side-to-side. The last thing I wanted to attempt was an extended ride with a suspect ankle.

So I sat on December 26th with the windows open, exposing a 69-degree, fresh, crisp, cloudless, Florida morning—perfect riding weather if you get my drift. And I was typing, instead of pedaling.

> "...riding is more than something *I do*. It's become a part of who *I am*."

My disappointment was tempered by two things: 1) the belief that my ankle would be well enough to ride the following day, and 2) the awareness that riding had become a genuine joy in my life, one worthy of celebration. I didn't start off as a cyclist; I never had the intention of becoming one. But there's no denying that getting on the bike, experiencing the freedom, the exhilaration of movement, the health benefits, the challenge to attain goals, the camaraderie I share with others, the shared experiences of riding with my wife ... it's such a significant part of my life now. As I reflect on what riding has become for me and the satisfaction it brings, it's abundantly clear that riding is more than something *I do*. It's become a part of who *I am*.

I don't know how many years I have left in this world, but I hope to spend a good portion of it in the saddle.

> "My hope for you is that leadership excellence becomes so vivid and real that you can't imagine ~~doing~~ being anything else."

I can't think of a more fitting topic for the final chapter and one that—hopefully—needs very little explanation as to why it's the shortest one in the book. My hope for you is that leadership excellence becomes so vivid and real that you can't imagine ~~doing~~ being anything else.

Your leadership setting could be anywhere: a company, your family, your unit, your shift, your associates and friends, your coworkers, strangers you meet in the subway. But in whatever circumstances Providence places you, live out your leadership opportunity to the best of your ability. Let leadership excellence become such a natural expression of your identity that it feels like home.

I wish you all the joy, satisfaction and gratification possible. Being a leader is a high calling, indeed.

Semper Incito: Enjoy the ride!

Put It in Motion

- **Think About Leadership as Something You Are, Not Just Something You Do.** Let it be a part of your identity, and enjoy the gratification that it can—and will—bring.

EPILOGUE –
CHARACTER AND LEGACY

*"The key to becoming an effective leader is
not to focus on making other people follow,
but on making yourself the kind of person
they want to follow."*
John Maxwell

You may have noticed something missing in this book. There's been no mention of a name that, until recently, would have been in the first sentence in any conversation about cycling and leadership: Lance Armstrong.

In the early stages of writing my manuscript, the truth finally came out on his long, sordid story. In an age where our only heroes are CG-steroided action movie characters, he was the genuine article. His story, so compelling, so personal and tangible, enthralled a nation and inspired so many—especially those who have lived with and through cancer. He was an icon of the American brand, embodying the things we aspire to: courage, getting back up, stronger, faster, brasher. He mainstreamed cycling, bringing untold thousands into the sport (myeself included). He gave hope to those who had lost it. And to those surviving families and friends of loved ones who didn't survive their war with cancer, he provided a way to do something about it.

"He settled for wins. He could have had a legacy."

He had the chance to do something special and to be so much bigger than seven Tour de France victories. He had the opportunity to influence millions of people and to be an inspiration to people who needed hope and a reason to overcome. His name could have become a rallying cry, a call to perseverance for generations to come.

Instead, he flushed it all away. He squandered an opportunity that Providence rarely provides. He bullied, blamed and attacked others to cover his own lies and deception, damaging the professional reputations of others to the point they could no longer follow their dreams. He vehemently denied the accusations for years. He marketed himself as the victim, looking right in the cameras to boldly plead his innocence—knowing all the while he was lying through his teeth.

He settled for wins.

He could have had a legacy.

> "Everyone wants to win; there's nothing really remarkable about that. It's what you are willing—or unwilling—to do to achieve victory that sets you apart."

This is not a rant against Lance or cheating in sports. It's much bigger than that. He's only one of a long list of people who swung and missed at a sure thing—a leadership home run. The temptation all leaders face, at one point or another, is to set our sights far too low and focus on the shiny win. To be so small-minded and self-oriented that winning is the limit of our vision.

Everyone wants to win; there's nothing really remarkable about that. It's what you are willing—or unwilling—to do to achieve victory that sets you apart.

Leadership excellence requires character. It's built on integrity: A soundness of spirit and a perspective that envisions more than your own interests. It survives through having deep roots—deep enough to keep you grounded when the winds of self-promotion blow. Without character, other people are expendable and mere stepping stones on the path to wherever it is you think you want to go.

Leadership is never just about you. The best leaders don't just succeed. They help others succeed. Only character allows you to see beyond yourself. Without it, you will forfeit the opportunity to impact others at a deeply profound level.

So where does character come from?

It comes from values. It comes from a belief system that is both bigger than you and beyond you. It comes from wisdom and the counsel of others, who are objective enough to see you as you really are, who are not looking to profit from their relationship with you and—most importantly—who have the courage to speak truth into your life. These things hold you accountable. They forge your character and give you the perspective you need to walk away from the temptations of self and expediency.

Personally speaking, my faith in Jesus Christ provides that system. I know there are rules of the game set by Someone bigger than me. I believe I'm only part of a larger story. My life and choices will be evaluated according to standards not of my creation and beyond the reach of my manipulation.

> "It's important, in my opinion, to have a faith that practices you— not the other way around."

Not that you have to be a person of faith to have character. And, to be sure, practicing a faith is no guarantee of living a life of character. It's important, in my opinion, to have a faith that practices you—not the other way around.

Wherever you are, I invite—counsel, challenge, encourage, appeal—you to secure your source of character. Decide where you will plant your roots and what kind of living nourishment you will seek to sustain you and keep you firmly planted.

It could very well be the most important and strategic leadership decision you ever make.

ABOUT THE AUTHOR

Damian Gerke is passionate about helping leaders get better. He is a learning and performance practitioner, a leadership coach and author. He has helped countless people in a variety of roles understand and apply the principles of effective leadership in practical, actionable ways. Damian has worked as an engineer in the aerospace industry, in vocational pastoral roles as an ordained minister and has led the learning and development initiatives at one of the leading third-party logistics services providers in North America. He is a Certified Professional in Learning and Performance (CPLP) through the Association for Talent Development.

Damian blogs regularly at DamianGerke.com, and you can also follow him on social media.

Made in the USA
Middletown, DE
23 September 2021

48047262R00106